Lloyd Jerome

Lloyd Jerome was born in Yorkshire, England in 1961, and whilst he may lay claim to growing up in a very green and pleasant part of the Yorkshire Dales, he took a very passive role in the gardening and farming that are now such a major part of his life. He is the third of five children, all of whom are emotionally close whilst being geographically distant.

He qualified as a dentist in Edinburgh, Scotland in 1985, and has worked and travelled in many countries in Australasia, Asia and Africa. He returned to the UK in 1991 and set up his own practice in Glasgow in 1993. The practice won awards for innovation and design, incorporating, as it did, an art gallery and bar into the premises, and virtual reality into the surgery.

In 2002 he married Laura, and, in 2005 they sold their house, the practice and many of their possessions, and migrated to the far north of New Zealand where they bought a small farm and a tiny house. They have every intention of staying there.

“Cricket By Candlelight” is his first book. It is by no means his last.

Cricket By Candlelight

by
lloyd jerome

First published in New Zealand in 2012 by Lloyd Jerome

First Edition.

For more information and images please go to:

www.lloydjerome.com

ISBN: 978-0-473-22495-0

To Laura, my muse, with all my love

Acknowledgements:

I'd like to thank a whole lot of people who have helped Laura and I achieve our own little slice of contentment, and, in the process, helped me write this book.

Mum and Dad for supporting me in all kinds of ways and for all your love.

Tom and Denise for being such wonderful in-laws!

Frank and Juen for being the best possible neighbours and friends, and especially for our first NZ Christmas.

R&V for your enthusiasm, friendship and employment.

N&S for being brilliant, and most supportive of friends.

Rod and Gilla for helping me bring the book to fruition, and for all your editing help.

Andrew, for designing the cover.

And to all our neighbours and friends in the far North for making this region the most wonderful home.

Thanks, all of you!

Prologue

Yesterday, in an act of glorious vandalism, I took a crowbar to the inside of a beautiful, early twentieth century wooden villa. Discussing the meaning of life with me was a plain-speaking eleven year old girl. She wielded a lump hammer with the strength of Pansy Potter. We made quite some mess, and it wasn't even my house.

Through a door in the next room Laura, my wonderful wife, was putting the finishing touches to a coat of paint. Elsewhere in the house, ten friends, adults and children, were starting to restore this wooden palace to its former glory. From time to time we glanced at the view down the inlet to Russell and the Bay of Islands. Each time we looked it whispered back to us: "this is one of the most beautiful views in the world".

Later, we dined on fresh fish and chips off newspaper. The dogs ate the scraps from below. Laura and I wondered, not for the first time, if we could have done a better job of removing ourselves from our stress-fuelled lives back in the UK. We suspected not.

So I'm going back to the start of it. I want to see where we went right.

Lloyd Jerome

Time to leave

There he is, the flash urbanite, in his early forties, driving down the long, sweeping bends in his newly acquired, very fast Audi saloon. A beautiful woman is by his side and the car journey from Glasgow out to the Loch Fyne Oyster Bar usually takes about an hour. They would have driven it in just thirty five minutes had it not been for the conscientious traffic police just beyond the "Rest-and-be-Thankful" pass. It's his third speeding ticket since he bought the car a few weeks ago and something tells him it might be time to slow down. But the something telling him this is not very loud and has to compete with all sorts of other voices, so consequently it goes unheard.

You might know the man. You'll certainly have seen him, or his female equivalent, relaxed, casually dressed (but not cheaply, heaven forbid), nice car, nice house, nice lifestyle (as the tabloids say) if you care to look. Nice life. Lucky, lucky bastard.

Of course, all is not as it seems. Here's what you don't see: car by Audi Finance. Clothes courtesy of Amex. Interior furnishings by Visa. Mortgage by soul-sold-to-the-devil. And that's just the tip of the iceberg (or in his case perhaps, the lollo rosso). By the time he's thought about all the other debts, (which he tries so terribly hard not to do) the ones his business has built up to make it so impressive to onlookers, he realises he's not just poor, he's broke. And if he stops working for a second, it'll all fall to bits. And he's not unusual. All over Britain and the developed world, people who live as richly, comfortably, and twice as long as robber-barons, pay more to finance companies in interest than they do to themselves. And why? Just to surround themselves with luxury. Yes, but why? Because they can, because everyone else does and because, temporarily, it feels very, very good.

Of course you don't feel sorry for him. You bloody well shouldn't. His predicament has been created by his choices. He's one of the lucky ones and, anytime he likes, he can pay all his debts. All he needs to do is sell everything he has and choose a life more impecunious. There is no other way out unless he wins the lottery, and he doesn't even play the damn lottery.

*****

Every time I saw a programme on TV discussing (in what always seemed a slightly patronising way) the perils of debt, I squirmed. I had enough debt that even in my seven-figure business, I could barely afford to stay afloat. The more of these media reminders I saw, the more my head spun. I didn't even know if my wife knew the full extent of my debt – I really didn't even know if I knew. I was a mess. I could still seem to be holding things together, my persona was more or less intact, but inside, I was a bit chaotic (my thesaurus informs me I should say, "completely fucked up"). I was a full-time dentist and part-time art gallery owner, as well as a full-time small business manager and the pressure was affecting my health. I really didn't want to wait and see how long it would take before I cracked. It was clear that I had to do something and, for the first time, the way forward, would not involve borrowing more money to "consolidate" the debts yet again. Even my home was mortgaged so deeply that I was an owned man. All the solutions seemed to be rather dispiriting and involved either making the business do even better, or by contrast, declaring bankruptcy. Neither extreme appealed, nor did the sensible "middle way" suggested by well-meaning experts. Even my accountant advised bankruptcy (so I stopped talking to him. I couldn't bear anyone reminding me that I might have a problem).

Meanwhile, I was not the only one with issues that needed attention. Laura is my wife and when we met she was a very dedicated teacher of children with behavioural difficulties (the ambiguity in this sentence is not accidental, he said, ducking, as a domestic projectile comes whistling past). She worked in a residential school, so her hours were akin to indentured servitude. She was (and is) beautiful, intelligent and humble (you can stop twisting my ear, now, darling). She comes from a very small, nurturing, close family and is passionately proud of her heritage; Scotland in general, and Aberdeen in particular (whereas I am from the North of England and was therefore a Scot by aspiration alone).

It became apparent that all was not well in the field of special-needs education. After twelve years of loyalty to her job, she woke up one morning to find that, quite literally, she could not bear to go to work. We had both heard of burn-out and always assumed it only happened to other people, but this was real and dramatic in its intensity. It was as if a phobia had materialised, suddenly and perfectly formed, and all thought of teaching rendered Laura completely shaken and anxious. Fortunately, she had an excellent doctor who had seen sufficient examples of this problem before to diagnose and treat her in a sympathetic and practical way, and not just reach for the prescription pad. Meanwhile, the school, probably with their own deep experience of this issue, behaved in entirely the opposite way and, for a while, made her life hell by demanding written explanations and aggressive discussions. Indeed, they only stopped their patently unreasonable behaviour when she made it very clear, and in writing, that she had no intention of suing the education department for putting undue pressure on her at work. Bloody hell, isn't that a great system? And so, with Laura at home and me at work, we started to gaze into the future, and became determined that it wouldn't just look like more of the same.

Laura and I had discussed selling up and moving away on a few occasions. These flights of fancy were usually whilst we were on holiday and we knew, really, that they were as fickle as time-share marketing. They would dissolve in the grey light of a Glasgow morning. We thought we knew what our ideal future might look like, but we had no way to divine how we might get there, nor even where "there" was.

In a break from our typically last minute tradition, we decided to book a holiday a year ahead. I'd been invited to a dental meeting in Vancouver, from there taking a cruise ship north to the icy seas of the Alaskan coast. As a holiday, it sounded like hell - hundreds of dentists on the one ship - but as a tax break, and somewhere interesting to go that both of us were keen to see, it sounded a reasonable idea. So we went online and, for the first time in our lives, booked a cabin on a cruise ship... but then, and not long afterwards (say thirty seconds) we looked at each other and said (in perfect unison):

"What if we went away somewhere wonderful and never came back?"

And the cat suddenly had one paw sticking right out of the bag.

Within a few hours we had covered a conversation that must have been lodged, fermenting in our minds for ages. It seemed so natural and logical that it was effortless. The theme was the same as the ones we had on holidays, the ones that look like time-share sales pitches, but this time the decision was no longer purely emotional, it was rational too. When that happens things change, and the present suddenly looks old and out of date, like the previous model iPod.

And so we played the "destination game" which, for us went something like this:

Me: "The Western Isles of Scotland?"

Laura: "What about them?"

Me: "We're playing the destination game."

Laura: "Oh, you should have told me."

Me: "We are playing the destination game."

Laura: "OK, the Western Isles; you'd have to set up your own practice from scratch, it'd be awfully quiet in the winter, but lovely in the summer."

Me: "But the whisky..."

Laura: "hmm... maybe not Isla, then. How about the Pyrenees?"

Me: "French or Spanish?"

Laura: "You tell me."

Me: “Beautiful mountains, lovely mountain people, delicious mountain food, but we’d need to learn French or Spanish.”

Laura: “I’m not sure I want to learn another language again. My Spanish is OK, but my French is merde.”

Me: “How about Australia?”

Laura: “Too hot, and all that stuff about bitey, poisonous animals!”

Me: “Otherwise perfect, then.”

Laura: “No. But New Zealand?”

Me: “New Zealand?”

Laura: “New Zealand.”

We: “New Zealand!”

(Bloody hell, any more of this and it might turn into a musical.)

But it really was almost as arbitrary as that. Of course, New Zealand is quite a big place, at least as large as Britain, so having narrowed down the destination to a country, we then had to decide where in New Zealand we’d like to live. In this regard, I had a slight advantage over Laura in that I’d been there before, fifteen years before. I don’t suppose it could have changed too much. Laura would have to make that interesting leap of faith by taking a one-way ticket to an unknown land in the antipodes. So some research was therefore needed. We looked at websites, pored over online real estate brochures, studied the climate, watched the exchange rate, applied for, and completed, reams of paperwork. We asked friends and their friends for opinions of their experiences and finally, after hours of in-depth investigation, I saw, in a book, an aerial photograph of the Bay of Islands.

"What do you think of that?" I asked, rhetorically.

"Looks lovely!" Laura replied less rhetorically.

"I would like to live there," I said, using no rhetoric whatsoever.

And then came the bombshell reply:

"Ok, let's do that, then!"

So our focus was narrowed down to that thin strip of the far north of New Zealand that juts out into the water, separating the Tasman Sea from the mighty Pacific Ocean, and wearing its climate in a relaxed, sub-tropical kind of way. Oddly, the far north of New Zealand was the one area I hadn't visited all those years ago when I took a month off from my peripatetic existence in Australia to have a peripatetic holiday there. We looked at the map, and I had a trawl through the phone book to gather phone numbers and email addresses for potential employers in Northland, as that part of New Zealand is called. We concentrated especially on those within a short distance of the Bay of Islands.

I wrote an email and copied it to all the addresses I could find. It was simple and to the point. Did they have, or know of someone who had, a vacancy for an experienced, enthusiastic dentist looking for a part-time job and if they did, could we come and meet them? Some people replied. Not many, but enough to get us excited. The first positive reply that came back arrived whilst I was at work. Laura forwarded it on to me:

"Yee Fucking Ha! I love you xxx" she wrote. Oddly, she sent the email back to Trevor, the Northland dentist who had sent it, instead of me. He said that he was very amused and, now that we've met, I believe him. It certainly didn't put him off wanting to meet us. Also, his son, who was on holiday in Scotland, visited and stayed with us (quite possibly to see just how odd we might be).

Most of the replies were from dentists in Whangarei, (usually pronounced Fangeray), Northland's main town. There was one reply from Kerikeri, which is actually in the Bay of Islands area and another hour's drive further north. But the reply from the Kerikeri dentist included the memorable phrase "...if we win you..." and gave us an invitation to stay with them. That was all I needed to hear. The cruise was cancelled, and the time set aside for that holiday became the dates for our job-seeking reconnaissance of Northland, staying, at first, with Trevor in Whangarei. All we needed was a residency visa. Oh, and vaccinations for the pets. And to sell the business. And the house. And to dispose of most of our possessions, and suddenly, a million overwhelmingly novel little things to do. By now it was February and we'd be visiting New Zealand in June.

June came round rather rapidly. Time really does contract when you are constantly doing new things. (I know that's nowhere nearly as concise as the usual cliché, but we were only having a modicum of fun, and time was still flying). Our migration paperwork and medicals went quite smoothly, helped by the fact that dentistry is in demand in rural areas and we weren't criminals. I had placed the flat with a very posh estate agency, and they seemed to be doing their utmost to find the least appropriate people to come and see it. As flats go, it was about as child-unfriendly as you could imagine; very white, sharp edged balustrades, ship's railings around a deep atrium, and a long tumble down a steel spiral staircase to the hardwood floor below! Ideal for a toddler, but only if it's a toddler you don't like very much. So, yes, by all means bring round plenty of young parents, that'll be splendid. One couple (without children) did like it. I knew they liked it, they came round seven times. But they didn't make us an offer. And then the housing market started to falter.

Meanwhile the business (a dental practice inside a busy art gallery) was also up for sale. Despite it being a little idiosyncratic, I was surprised to learn that it was attracting plenty of attention in the dental world, and I had offers galore. Some of them were laughable (and I love a good laugh, me) but one of them was the asking price, which amazed me. In fact, the offer was so good I thought it must be too good to be true. But no, the solicitors were doing their usual business, contracts were being drawn up and, before long and well before expected, I had a buyer! And so, with mixed emotions and, for the first time that I could remember since my feckless youth, a possibility of freedom from debt, and suddenly it was June. Our trip to New Zealand was upon us.

I love travel and holidays. But, for the last few years, every holiday had been marred by the spectre of deepening debt. For every day I was away from the business, we were spending without earning, and it was this feeling, rather than any real love for a protestant ethic that had driven me into workaholism. I toiled hard because that was what was keeping the credit card sharks from the door. But this holiday would be different. To start with, I was really looking forward to seeing New Zealand again after all those years and, on top of that, because Laura had never been there, I was excited to see what she made of it. Moreover, the holiday had a purpose beyond just travel.

However, there was one item on our pre-holiday agenda we had both overlooked, probably because we both knew it would cause some emotional distress, and that nettle had to be grasped soon. We really had to discuss our plans with our families. Our first stop was Laura's Mum and Dad. It didn't go well. Initially, Laura's mother was sure that the move was my idea, and the thought of losing her only daughter to the antipodes was unpalatable. It took her many tears and long phone calls before she was convinced that Laura was an equal partner and willing accomplice in this plan. And it didn't help that our explanation for the "why New Zealand?" question was that it looked nice in photos!

My parents took a slightly different view:

"Of course, we'll miss you, but we're surprised you haven't done this years ago" was their consensus. But tempered with "I don't suppose we'll come and visit though, it's far too far away for that!" Thankfully, this turned out to be incorrect.

My closest friend (who was my best 'man' at our wedding) had one piece of advice for Laura:

"Don't let Lloyd work too hard" she said "otherwise, there's no difference between here and there. Work is the same all over the world once it becomes routine".

We hadn't expected unbridled delight in our imminent departure, but it was difficult coming to terms with the idea that perhaps we might be toying a little whimsically with our future. We had no right to expect that our families would understand our motives and process for this sudden life-changing decision when we didn't fully understand them ourselves. But despite all this, it still felt like the right thing to do. And then we were on our way.

Arrival in NZ

The low clouds parted as we descended towards Auckland. Our first sight of land as we rapidly lost height was the west coast. Glittering black sandy beaches were backed by intensely green bushland, and if there were any houses there, they blended invisibly into the landscape. It was exciting but it was tempered with the odd, rather surreal sensations that accompany the end of two days of near-constant travel. So we felt happy to be arriving, but detached from our feelings at the same time. A bit like when you wake up within a dream and know that you are still dreaming.

Our passports had just been renewed, and were the proud bearers of a page-sized blue sticker that declared us residents of New Zealand. To our delight, at passport control, the officer looked at the stickers, looked at us, beamed, and said: “Welcome to New Zealand!” We breezed through the rest of that maze of officialdom and conveyor belts that is an international airport, floating on what felt like a cloud of elation (but was probably what the experts call jet lag).

A very helpful man, armed with paperwork, maps and an inimitable Kiwi drawl, showed us to our little rental car and explained to us, gravely, that the road north through

Auckland is confusing, poorly-signed and counterintuitive (in fact I think he said "she's a total bugger to get through") and warned us of the idiosyncrasies of driving in New Zealand; the (now defunct) "give way to drivers turning right" rule and the (still in use) "all other drivers on the road are idiots" rule. And how right he was: before they get in a car, the lovely, down to earth, friendly people of this land take a pint of whatever it was that Dr Jekyll was drinking on that fateful night. We passed through Auckland, the weather going from stormy to glittering and clear, and we were heading north towards Whangarei. It occurred to me that I should probably phone Trevor, our first contact and potential employer, to announce our arrival and get some directions to find him. So we stopped at a cafe in the Dome Valley for a bite to eat and a coffee. And this highlights the powerful psychotropic effects of jet lag; we pronounced the food and drink "the best ever" and declared that this café would be our wayside stop to and from Auckland for evermore. Later that month we would pass through this cafe again, and see it for what it probably was the first time, weak coffee, floury milkshakes and white flaccid chips. We've never been back again! So we navigated our way north, seeing and marvelling at the novelty of it all, knowing that it wouldn't be long before the newness of things, the shape of manuka trees, ponga ferns and nikau palms, the variety of wooden houses, the brightness of the sky over the Hauraki gulf, would all become familiar, domestic and nigh on invisible.

In truth, I should probably not have been driving. After two days of travel, lack of sleep, moving swiftly from summer to winter and confusing day lengths, I must have been a liability as my judgement would certainly have been impaired. Fortunately, and more by luck, my uselessness never achieved its full potential. Unwittingly we drove on and arrived without incident, despite the fact that I, the driver, probably slept for most of the journey! We met up with Trevor for the first time. He's a granite man is Trevor, not really chatty (but he likes a good joke) and although he doesn't say much, he's very easy to read. Honestly, I remember little from those first few hours, but I am indebted to him for lending us his family bach which was about another forty minutes picturesque drive away, and right on the water. (A bach is a holiday beach house and is pronounced "batch")

We arrived and, without even coming close to unpacking, we slept. We awoke to a sub-tropical winter morning. Cold, clear, bright and so beautiful I may even have shed a tear. Out at Whangarei Heads we were overlooked by closed up holiday houses and the lightest smattering of year-round residents. The tide was in, the water only a few metres away, glittering and dappled by the light through the branches of innumerable pohutukawa trees. Feeling cold, drowsy but excited we rushed about pretending to do things and gradually made some sense of our new surroundings.

"A few friends of ours are having supper tomorrow night, would you come and join us?" asked Trevor the next day; "we'll meet at the restaurant at half past five, if that's OK with you."

I must have been feeling a little groggy from the sleep, because I could swear he said half past five. I phoned him back:

"Sorry to be a pest - what time was that again?"

"About half past five," he confirmed.

Maybe they get together for drinks quite early first. So we arrived at the restaurant and a party of about eight of us sat down for supper quite promptly, half way through the afternoon. The conversation was lively and spirited, with a great deal of banter to which I felt I couldn't contribute, since I knew little of New Zealand's sport and politics. By eight o'clock it was dark, we were saying farewell, and we went home to bed. The food was excellent, the company very pleasant, but I realised, in an odd way, that this country was more foreign to me than I had expected - and I should have expected it to be very foreign. Was I, Mr Metropolitan, to be in bed by nine? Good lord, this might take more adaptation than I thought.

The first week in Northland passed in a bit of a blur,

meeting the dentists of Whangarei and making inevitable snap judgements and comparisons. There was the enthusiastic dentist with his lovely young family, proudly Jewish, with a pet pig called "Kosher" and a brand new practice, still growing, to whom I could offer much advice (he knew me by small-world reputation before we met) but little prospect for work. And then there was a couple who, like us, were keen to make a break with the past, sell up and, in their case, travel around Australia in a luxury motor home. Keen as they were to find a buyer for their practice, they introduced us to their staff as the "Scottish couple who've come to buy our business". A fire the which I had no desire to re-ignite, having just jumped out of the frying pan. We were invited round for a meal on their beautiful rural property and they gave us a banquet from the barbecue. But, despite it being delicious, we were both consumed by an extraordinary attack of flatulence which, if suppressed, led to the most extreme stomach pain. We made bizarre excuses and left suddenly, giggling, and releasing huge magenta bubbles of gas into the poor hire car as soon as we were out of earshot. We could simply have said no to their kind sales pitch, but our guts were more eloquent than our mouths. "Alimentary, my dear Watson".

At the end of the week we phoned the couple in Kerikeri who had offered us the possibility of work in their new practice, just opened, and who seemed very enthusiastic. They had very kindly suggested we come and stay with them and have a look. So, on yet another sunny morning, we found ourselves driving up the long straight main road, bordered for the most part by exceptionally tall hedges of bamboo and trimmed Leylandii. On our way we caught glimpses of houses with orchards beyond. Following the directions, we arrived for our first meeting with Wayne and Millie, the lovely couple who had talked of “winning” us.

It was clear from the start that Kerikeri was going to appeal to us. Millie, Wayne and their family of three young girls were so welcoming, so accommodating and helpful, and so much like long-lost friends that we were powerless to resist. They seemed to feel the same way, and their enthusiasm about their home was so contagious and charming that we instantly fell in love with the place. Kerikeri is a fast-growing town, making the transition from sleepy orchard town and haven for retirees, to a young, fashionable and modern centre with smart cafés, designer shops and (since we’ve been here) a beautiful new cinema. We didn’t take long to realise that we would rather be here than Whangarei, and it only took a day or two more to discover that we’d rather be here than anywhere else in the world. Once that decision was made, we had to negotiate an employment contract with our new friends. It went something like this:

"I'd like to work three days a week, and I'm happy to be paid fifty percent of my gross" says I.

"Arr" says Millie, (who, for sake of this made-up dialogue, is training to be a pirate) "that be the terms, then. Sign here in ye blood and we be ownin' ye".

And so the job was won. And we were won. And we were completely won over. It all happened really fast. Sometimes everything clicks into place, and the clockwork was so well oiled that we were suddenly in Kerikeri, with friends, with time on our hands, and all our plans for the reconnaissance to Northland settled well ahead of time. So to occupy ourselves, especially as Wayne and Millie were very experienced in the world of real estate, we thought we might do what we had promised ourselves we wouldn't do, and look at houses for sale. The whole point of that promise to each other was so that we wouldn't fall in love with an area before we were certain that it was the part of New Zealand that was going to be our new home. Our vague plan had been to rent somewhere for a few months and then, if the area didn't fulfill its initial appeal, we could cut our ties and move on. And yet, just as I saw that aerial photo of the Bay and knew I was looking at our future, we both felt, in an entirely emotional way, that we had arrived at our new home.

Laura had a good idea of the kind of house she wanted.

Back in Glasgow, our flat was entirely my design, planned before we'd even met. It was grand, spacious, extravagant, and architecturally exciting. But despite being beautiful and exotic, it wasn't Laura's idea of heaven. I was very happy for our new home to be somewhere Laura and I could both love, and her tastes are simple, pastoral, and very "country cottage", which perhaps is surprising for a lass who grew up and always lived in cities. Our brief to the billions of real estate agents in Kerikeri was straightforward: we want a small house, preferably wooden, preferably old, preferably painted white! It has to have a garden big enough for a dog to run around,

"...and it must be less than this price", we said, self-consciously revealing a figure to the agent..

"Well!" said Rolf, a migrant from Germany, a windsurfing expert and our favourite estate agent of the seemingly countless ones, "I think that might be impossible! I will show you some places we have on our books, my dear (I think he meant Laura), but these villas that you are wanting are not so common in Kerikeri and we don't see many of them on the market. Also, the price is very low."

He took us on a "tiki-tour" of the area (this is a New Zealand expression meaning a drive around the place – at breakneck speed, in his case) showing us what was on the books, and pointing out places of interest as he went. We started out responding with typical British politeness, murmuring words like “interesting” and “mm!” and making rude faces to each other when his back was turned. In time (and Rolf was happy to devote plenty of it to us, with no sense of pressure or hard-sell) we took to scanning the house from the outside, looking at each other, and then simply saying no to Rolf’s latest offering. We saw perfect houses in entirely the wrong location, we saw awful houses in perfect locations, and we saw at least one house that was smelly, ugly and just wrong. That’s when we dumped the polite facade. After two days of fruitless tiki-ing, we were out of options, and we’d seen nothing that we really liked. This came as a total surprise to us all, as there had seemed to be so many potential places available within our price range when we looked at the real estate websites. But we hadn’t reckoned with the distances here; places that looked local to us from our Glasgow vantage point were about forty five minutes drive away, and whilst that didn’t seem unreasonable to our rush hour hardened sensibilities, it didn’t take into account the Northland roads, the Kiwi drivers and the cultural notions of distance that assumes that, with so much land and so few people, you’d be mad to drive more than a few minutes to work. But that was fine with us, we’d only just started looking, and we’d have plenty of time to search for our perfect home once we were settled in a rental property on our return, whenever that was going to be.

Two days before we were due to leave Kerikeri we were in Rolf's office when the receptionist walked in, saw us and said:

"I've just seen the perfect place for you two!"

It was an old, small farm that had been subdivided into two parts, but had been, until today, on the market as a single title. After seeing no buyers interested in the whole property, the owners had decided to remarket the place as two small farms, each with its own house. The receptionist had a picture of the house she thought we'd like. It was a tiny, hundred year old weatherboard house, with a corrugated iron roof, two windows eye-like on either side of the nose of a door. Just like the one in so many children's drawings. It looked cute, it looked run down and it looked possible. But the land - it stood in twenty two acres of farmland, about twenty two times more than we wanted. Perhaps we could sell the land? Apparently not.

"So when can we go and see it?" Laura exclaimed.

Rolf had seen that expression before:

"Now is a good time for me, my dear, I'll phone the owners and see if that's ok with them".

It was, and we followed Rolf out of the office and said we'd follow him in our car if he led the way.

"Are you all right driving on gravel roads?" he asked.

"No problem!"

And within moments we'd reached the gravel, at which point Rolf Gelb, estate agent and Teutonic rally driver, shot ahead, taking the corners with opposite lock as appropriate. Only three kinds of car can go that fast on dirt roads. Four wheel drive cars, rally cars and rental cars. He was in the former and, fortunately, we were in the latter. Fifteen minutes later and covered in dust, we reached the highway, heart pumping, and completely lost. We looked around and we were in a different landscape entirely. The tall hedges and orchards had gone, and instead there were old European trees, poplars, elms and oaks, grey and crumbly dry stone walls and, in every direction on the near horizon, volcanic cones whose smoothness spoke of years of extinction. And all so green!

We crunched up a drive with grass growing down the middle of the track, through a wisteria-choked gate, and into a gravel yard bounded by cute but shabby buildings. As soon as we staggered out of the cars we were greeted, not only by two little dogs, but also by a sense of serenity and gentle calm. Alex, the owner, came out of the cottage in traditional New Zealand winter farmer's garb of shorts, teeshirt and gumboots. He welcomed us and we started to wander round the farm, he and Rolf chatting amiably, the dogs zooming around the paddocks in some kind of "find the smelly cow pat" game and we, lagging a few steps behind and grinning uncontrollably.

"Whatever you do, don't make it too obvious if we do want to buy this place" I cautioned my foolishly beaming wife. "I have no idea how we could manage twenty two acres, and we don't know much about gardening, never mind farming" I added, before I noticed that I too was smiling like an eighties dance badge (the yellow smiley face.) Back in the real world, and five steps ahead of us, Rolf and Alex were discussing things like the cost of fencing, what building repairs might be needed, and how well the ground had coped with the recent heavy rainfall. So prosaic. It took us about forty minutes to wander around the property and get back to the house. It took us about a thousandth of that time to fall in love with it. We had conveniently inserted ourselves into the picture, with dogs running around, cattle in the paddocks, and the huge and graceful oak tree dappling the shade for a garden picnic. And before we'd even seen inside the house, it had to be ours.

In fact, the house was a little unprepossessing. Crowded with heavy, dark antique furniture, it seemed impossibly small for a family of four and if we'd seen it first, it might have made us a little more trepid. But the farm had worked some kind of voodoo on us, and the cottage was far more beautiful in our mind's eye than reality. It just didn't seem to matter. This is what they call 'falling in love' with a property, and wisdom counsels against it. Despite my stern admonition, Laura blurted:

“I love it! Please can we buy it?”

Alex was delighted, and such a gentleman that he showed no sign of the glint in the eye that suggests a rapidly inflating price tag. We drove away, this time, and at my request, on the sealed road, and arrived back to the office. The conversation in the car had been predictably enthusiastic, no second view was necessary, we should put in a conditional offer. I tried to get cold feet and imagine what we might do with such a large acreage, how we could improve the cottage with limited funds, what we would use all the outbuildings for, and generally attempted to feel intimidated by the scale and suddenness of the decision. But to no avail, no matter how hard I tried, the feeling of tranquillity that pervaded the place overcame any pessimism. I smiled and knew we’d found the right spot.

Rolf drew up preliminary documents for the sale and Millie helped us find a solicitor who wouldn’t cost a fortune to do the conveyancing. And the next day, it was time for us to head south to Auckland. Before we left the area, we thought we’d drive past the house, just for another brief look. It’s crazy how we can commit to spending so much money without too much of a second thought. Sometimes, I swear I’ve spent more time buying a present than it took to choose the house. So we drove along the highway and stopped on the verge next to the tumbledown volcanic stone wall. There was the farm, partially hidden by young trees, and beckoning us back. And just as Laura stared to cry, partly because she didn't want to leave it, but also for the sheer overwhelming emotional high we'd developed in the last few days, Alex saw us, waved and came over to invite us in for a cup of tea. Laura sucked the tears back in and we took a last, lingering visit to the cottage before we left Northland and then New Zealand.

And damn it, we left all the presents we had bought for our friends and family in the boot of the rental car.

Back in Scotland again

On a blustery but warm morning in early August, Laura and I were sitting on the shore of Loch Voil, cooking lamb chops on the barbecue, watching Bob the dog pretending to amuse himself (he really needs our input) and silently and separately wondering when we would make that final, last brave step, and dare to buy the one-way tickets that speak of a real commitment to our future. We were already missing New Zealand, and were a little anxious that, in some inexplicable way, it might stop existing if we don't get back there soon. We knew the practice was selling, we even had a proposed date for the deal to go through. The house seemed, suddenly, to be terribly overcapitalised and far more of a specialised item than we imagined. Design magazines loved it but viewers seemed nonplussed. Could we really wait for months to find the right buyer and, with the business sold, what work would we need to do to keep ourselves away from the spectre of bankruptcy (or at least repossession)?

So there we were, sitting in one of Scotland's most lovely places (of which it can boast a few) distracted and a little fretful when suddenly, as seems often to be the case, clarity descended, and the problem became a simple one:

"If we booked our tickets to Auckland for, say, the end

of September", said Laura, cautiously, "and you had a job to go to when we get to New Zealand, then couldn't we just pay our mortgage from there until the house sells?"

Of course, this was heresy. To leave Glasgow with our biggest millstone still hanging round our necks - at the very least it would cost a fortune in excess baggage. But, all of a sudden, it was a possibility. The sensible part of it was that we were going to where the work was. The madness was that we were leaving the house to sell, and hope to service the debt from the other side of the world. But even before we left Loch Voil we realised that we had just turned a corner. The tension that we were feeling, that not-quite-ready-to-leave sensation had evaporated and all of a sudden, we were on our way. That evening, excited and absolutely sure of ourselves, we booked one-way tickets, Glasgow to Auckland with Cathay Pacific, and, as a present to ourselves, and in an attempt to help Laura hate flying a little less, we booked Business Class seats. And, as of September 30th we were no longer residents of the United Kingdom! Immediately, with a clear decision made, things seemed so much more straightforward. I discovered that I could freeze the mortgage payments for six months, so then the flat could sell at its own speed. We had until January before that would become a real crisis. Once again, with a simple conversation, and a decision made, we reeled in the future and made it part of the present. And it felt very, very good!

Light of heart, we returned to Glasgow, and planned the move in all its finality. The practice was good as sold, with the new owner taking over the business in two weeks, which gave us about six weeks to pack up, zoom around the UK to say goodbye to all our friends and family and finally drop off Bob and the two cats to the specialist animal transport company before we flew south. It would be a light, breezy and cathartic few weeks, in which my biggest challenge would be to become accustomed to not micro-managing my business, and not even going to work!

But despite our enthusiasm, and almost boundless energy for the plans, a dark and ominous cloud settled upon us that extracted all the joy and levity from the next few weeks. The woman who had bought the practice from me was a tiny, pretty, and energetic young dentist, whose wide-eyed enthusiasm appeared entirely guileless. She seemed like the ideal person to take up the reins of a business that, for the past fourteen years, had been my proud obsession. She planned to launch her takeover of the practice with a big family party and religious blessing on Friday night, prior to her first day of work on the following Monday. That Friday, as I packed up all my possessions, and looked at the premises for possibly the last time, she approached me and said:

"I'm really sorry about this, but I can't pay for the

practice as I'd planned!" I stood, dumbfounded, with my brain really not accepting this last sentence.

"But everything is signed...the deal's already done."

Somewhere, in a small part of my mind, I was thinking, "I knew this would happen; it all seemed too good to be true". I said out loud:

"What happens now, then?"

"You can sue me if you want" she murmured, more embarrassed than apologetic.

I looked at my shoes in disbelief. They had never seemed browner. I have no idea why. I didn't want to sue her; I just wanted the last minute of my life to be imaginary.

"I have to talk to my solicitor." Was all I could think to say, rather unimaginatively. No quickwitted ripostes, no off the cuff solutions. Way deep down, I was probably thinking: "Mummy!"

I spoke to the solicitor:

"How can this happen? Everything was finalised!" I remonstrated, hoping that an appropriate level of anguish might change everything back to normal.

"Until you have the money in your account, it's all just promises" said Mark, my tall, young and praeternaturally wise counsel. "These things happen," he added.

"But don't panic, I'll see what's going on and let you know what we do next. Have a good weekend!"

Oddly enough, we didn't go to the party and blessing. We didn't have a good weekend. We agonised. We second-guessed Monday. We didn't know what to think. So we thought of all the bad things we could. On Monday morning, I could see it in my mind's eye, she would be there, using my chair, treating my patients, with my staff, and I felt robbed, duped out of my practice, betrayed. Beyond that, I grew childishly fearful of the tidal-wave of debt that had, just for the minute, been frozen overhead, poised to come crashing down on us if all the promises that I had made to my creditors could not be kept on Monday morning. That weekend was spent in a daze of negative thoughts. Too much supposition, alleviated only by dog walking. Of course, it rained incessantly.

On Monday morning, as early as I dared, I went to see Mark, who was ready and rested after what was probably, for him, a routine and pleasant weekend. How could that be possible? Was he not psychic? I had options, but, until he could speak to "that woman's" solicitor, he wouldn't know what would be most practical. Sure, I could take legal action, I could take my practice back, I could put it back on the market and find another buyer, I could contact all the other dentists who seemed interested a few months ago, or I could rent the business to her until such time as she could pay as agreed.

"Wait! What was that last option? That sounds possible.

Doesn't it?"

I saw a straw and grasped it. And that turned out to be the path we took. Every week we asked the same questions over and over again:

"Was the funding in place? How much longer would this situation continue? Why was no one letting us know what was going on? How is this even possible; surely avoiding this is what contracts are for? Why doesn't anyone else care?"

Sadly, Bob the dog didn't know many of the answers. But he did offer to cock his head to one side when we asked them, and lean his full weight against me when I sighed. All the joy was inexorably drained from our final weeks, and any attempt to spend this time in playful departure with our closest friends became impossible, a piece of bitter ash in my mouth. My resentment for "that woman" grew as our timetable for leaving began to seem more and more like a hasty retreat from mounting debt. In fact, the scenario that I had held at the back of my mind in my bleakest moments, that of running away from bankruptcy, seemed to be catching up with us. I wanted to make a clean break, to arrive in a new land without the extra baggage of the debt and the guilt that seemed to so much a part of each other. And so, with leaden and intensely brown shoes, we plodded towards the departure gate, our questions unanswered, and our future less certain.

The flight was a breeze, and we arrived in Auckland feeling a bit spun around but in excellent mood. All the gloom and anxiety of the last few weeks seemed to evaporate in the glare of the antipodean sun. Wayne and Millie had arranged with their old friends in Devonport to put us up for a couple of days in their sleepout so we picked up the same rental car (and the chocolates we had carelessly left in the boot two months ago!) and drove to their house in the early morning traffic. The weather was warm and bright and we felt curiously at home or, at the very least, well within our comfort zone. Devonport, one of the oldest suburbs of Auckland, is right on the water, a short ferry ride to the city centre. It's full of Victorian villas that look like the rich, posh aunties of the one we had fallen in love with up north. Ralph and Yvonne lived in one of these beautiful houses with their three phenomenally ungrateful children. We arrived very early in the morning and, rather than disturb anyone, we snuck into their "sleepout" (a popular New Zealand term for a converted shed, garage, hut - anything intended to put up temporary guests), looked at the bed, and collapsed in a sleepy heap. We woke at a more reasonable time, about three hours later, oddly refreshed. Before we had left, Laura had arranged on the Internet to look at a car very similar to the one she had in Glasgow, so we phoned the garage and went off to find out what it's like to buy a car in New Zealand. As it turns out the answer is–easy! The avuncular car salesman, Jeff, seemed genuinely interested in us and what we wanted from a car. He didn't seem anything like a real salesman:

"So whereabouts have you come from?" he asked.

And when he discovered that we'd come over from Scotland, he was quick to remind us of the beauty of the land we'd left far behind so recently and, as is entirely normal for New Zealanders, to point out that he too had some Scottish ancestors. And, no, we didn't know them. We spoke of our journey, our plans for the future, the beauty of Northland, the rising price of fuel, the best way to drive off-road and more. I was a little suspicious at first, assuming that all this chat would presage some hidden costs in the buying of the car but, in less than an hour, we owned a ten year old Jeep wagon, and that time included arranging a bank transfer. So we took the rental car back a day early and proudly drove PIXCAT back to Devonport (the registration number can be any six letters or numbers you want as long as no one else has them). And then we slept again.

In case anyone might think otherwise, the car may be old, and the salesman might have seen us coming from the other side of the world, but the Jeep is still going strong. The odd problem we had when we first tried to put it into four wheel drive was solved on the phone by Jeff who said that if it turned out to be a real issue, he would be prepared to fix it at his own expense.

"The last owner of the car was a catholic priest. I don't think he took the car off the road in its lifetime, so the four wheel drive might be a bit sticky" he explained.

"If you use it a wee bit, and shift back and forth into gear, the car should be sweet. If it still gives you grief, take it to a garage up north and give them my number. I'm sure she'll be right!"

This, it turned out, is a pattern that would repeat itself until we understood that it is normal here. That buying an expensive necessity involves dealing with people who actually take an interest in us, and are so guileless in their dealings that it is OK to trust them. How cynical and jaded I must have seemed when I first arrived.

After a day to recover and have a wander around and to eat with and enjoy the friendship of our hosts, we drove north to Kerikeri. This was the second time we'd driven this route, and the first time without chronic exhaustion. It's a beautiful drive, the highlight of which has to be the crossing of the Brynderwyn Hills. There is the sudden unveiling of a very long view of the Pacific Ocean breaking on one white beach after another, separated by headlands all the way to the biggest promontory at Whangarei Heads. Inland lie smooth rolling green hills and tiny rural towns. The sky is so huge that it defies European explanation; it still makes my heart leap when I see it in any weather and on this morning it was bright, sunny, clear and almost too breathtaking to relate. It was that feeling of coming home, but home as yet was an adventure in itself.

Up in Kerikeri, Millie, Wayne and the three children were all waiting for us so that they could show us to our rental cottage, called “Morne Fendue”, which they were quite familiar with as it used to be their home! It was as cute as we had imagined and, through that odd bewilderment that comes with long distance travel, before the mind has time to catch up with the body, we ambled around the field and cottage with a growing sense of delight. The cottage was comfortable, with the shabby-chic feeling of faded luxury that can only be achieved by not employing a professional interior designer. The surrounding steeply sloping garden led the eye to the reed ponds of a water bird sanctuary and the blue-green hills beyond. We sat on the deck and just gazed and grinned, until we realised that the sun was so intense that we might be getting sunburn! We drove into Kerikeri to have a look around, and remind ourselves why we wanted to live here. It’s a busy small town with a very open feel to the main street and a sense of newness that many smaller American towns have, but also a feeling of long-established gentleness that will be familiar to anyone who has lived in a citrus-growing area. And Kerikeri oranges are famed for their sweetness. Citrus trees need the same weather as we do. Not too hot (hardly ever above thirty degrees Centigrade) and not too cold (only the slightest frost). They need rainfall, but not too often the tropical deluges that would rot their roots and our books. Historically, when the early Pakeha (that's the Caucasian) settlers got to work on it, Kerikeri (which means "dig dig" in Maori) was orchards as far as the eye could see. Now, although many orchards remain, they are interspersed with houses of every style, from the old kauri villa to the very contemporary steel, plastic and glass constructions that modern New Zealanders love. Everyone wants their own "section" (plot of land) and until very recently, there was more than enough space to accommodate that.

Now, however, Kerikeri is one of the fastest growing New Zealand towns and, heavens above! people might have to drive fifteen minutes to get from their property to get into town. Over the next few days we rapidly became familiar with the Fishbone café and the internet booths next door. The cottage had no phone and was out of range of our mobiles, so Kerikeri was our link to the rest of the world, and after depending on the 'net for so long for all our communication across the world, it did feel as if our umbilical had been cut when we saw "no signal".

We had left Glasgow on the date we had planned months ago, but no one on whom we were financially dependent (like the people buying our home or business) seemed to care. So a new routine became established. E-mails to solicitor, family and friends were daily occurrences. It was without any drama or warning that our Glasgow house sold within two days of our migration and the first rock, that we'd been aware of, sitting on our shoulders, suddenly vanished. However, the payment for the dental practice still hadn't been made, so it wasn't until much later that the spectre of debt really stopped haunting us. But we had other things to do, and the distance to Scotland now rendered most of our previous worries abstract.

A new concern started to bear down on us. The deadline we had arbitrarily given to the real estate agent for buying the farm was fast approaching, and since I had assumed that we would need to use the money from the business, it now seemed to be a fading hope that it would become our new home. I had made friends at the bank. This is not a difficult process. Within a day, everyone seemed to know us by our first name and the manager, clearly near her maternity leave, seemed genuinely interested when I explained to her what was important to us, namely raising enough funds quickly to buy the farm, and then paying off as little as possible, assuming that the dental practice would be paid for very soon, wiping out the debt. I'd spent too much time with bank managers in Scotland and, without exception, they were all quite schizoid, charming and cheerful when I had money to invest, dour and humourless when I needed help from them. But Karen, our angel of the high street, was cast from a very different mould. And so, Angela, our new solicitor, Karen the bank manager, Rolf the estate agent and Mark, my solicitor in Scotland, all contacted each other with the pieces of paper they needed. Faxes sped back and forth. At one time the bank manager even was spied running (I repeat, that's a heavily pregnant bank manager, running) across the street to bring us a confirmation document before close of business. Within two days we had the funds in place and Darroch Cottage was ours! I'd never experienced anything like it, and it brought a smile to our faces to see everyone so complicit in ensuring that all went smoothly. Now, of course I know that this is normal for New Zealand, in fact everyone here assumes that this is how you do business. It took me a little while to work out exactly what is different in the approach to business taken here. But in fact, it's simple. Generally, and with good reason, people trust each other. I'm sure that there are plenty of exceptions to this, but in our experience this is the rule.

A week after we arrived, we had cause to nip down to Auckland with great excitement, despite the seven hour round trip. Bob the dog, and Pixie and Binky, the cats, were arriving and needed to be cleared through customs before we could deliver them to their new paradise. We couldn't wait to see them. I know it sounds awfully sentimental, but we'd not have moved to New Zealand if we couldn't bring our pets with us. So off we drove, wondering what kind of journey the animals had endured, and what state they'd be in after such a break from their normal life. Following directions from the customs department, we arrived at a nondescript warehouse within the airport sprawl. We found an office and a bubbly young customs officer met us:

"There's a fair bit of paperwork to do, I'm afraid!" she said, knowing that this wouldn't be the last time she'd say that today.

"We're just happy that we can pick up the animals" we countered, and off we went, to walk as fast as possible, due to our excited anticipation, to the international terminal to find another office and deliver the sheaf of papers she'd just given us. After some searching, and an almost comedic slo-mo race with another devoted pet owner who was completing the same tasks as us (neither of us wanted to be so rude as to actually look as if we were rushing, but we knew that there was only one person to deal with the bureaucracy) we had all the stamped papers and we trotted, breathlessly, back to the original warehouse. In fact we were so excited, neither of us made moan of the ridiculous distance between the two offices. And there were Bob and the cats, still in the crates that had been custom-made for them in the UK. We opened the box with Bob in it and he shifted towards us looking rather subdued. Suddenly, he realized who we were! He leapt forward, his tail wagging his whole body, his mouth in his widest grin. A week of isolation and dark transportation was behind him, and his Kiwi life was about to begin. Of course, he had no inkling of what changes we had made to his future. The cats were more circumspect, and we couldn't let them out until we got home for fear that they might run off forever.

Just north of Auckland is a small town called Orewa, and beyond that, a beach right next to the old highway. We stopped, let Bob out, and wandered down to the water. Bob had a quick sniff about, did an enormous shit (which, of course, we bagged and disposed of properly) and leapt into the sea. His first dip in the Pacific. He was just delighted, running up and down, constantly looking at us (as if to check that we weren't going to vanish again), before, happier then ever, wet and smelling of sheepskin, he leapt back in the car. The cats mewled in irritation (and envy), and we headed north. Bob loved his new temporary home, and, apart from the bizarre effects of jet lag (whereupon he would try to get us up to play with him at two in the morning and collapse into deep sleep in the middle of the day) he settled in very quickly. The cats were slower to find equilibrium, alternating between being very clingy and suddenly feral, and we kept them in the house for much longer than we had originally thought necessary. Then just as they were getting the hang of it all, it was time to leave "Morne Fendue" and move into our new home.

Settling in

The far north of New Zealand is sub-tropical; it lies approximately thirty five degrees south and boasts a very gentle climate. Before the arrival of people (the first Maori settlers of the country arrived, it's reckoned, some time between six hundred and one thousand years ago) one of the main features of the northern landscape was the massive conifer known as Kauri. These behemoths of the arboreal world vie with the famous Giant Redwoods of north-west America, and the Tasmanian Mountain Ash for the title of biggest tree in the world. Sadly, their enormous size and the straightness of their trunks was their downfall, and these days few really large specimens are left and some of these are so revered that they're individually named.

The legacy of the Kauri lives on, for not only are these trees now a protected species but also the beautiful houses that were built from the felled giants remain to this day and many have been lovingly restored. These kauri villas have had a varied history and are dear to the hearts of New Zealanders, although many would prefer not to live in them! Typically the last true kauri villas were built in about 1920, although the style of villa can still be commissioned and built today. They were a Victorian design and are usually recognised by their simple shape and complex decoration. High ceilinged with small rooms, they are commonly thought of as dark, draughty, difficult to heat, and damp. Perhaps we bought an exception, for Darroch Cottage is now a really cute, tiny house with a big, deep deck and veranda. The heating is only needed in winter (and not every day) and a well stocked woodshed is enough for a whole year's fuel supply. Our little villa was originally built in the Northland city of Whangarei as a railway worker's cottage and transported to its present position on the back of a truck a few years ago. It looks as if it's been here since it was built and feels solid as anything. More importantly, it feels as if it's where we've always lived, and is as comfortable as a favourite old shoe. In short, it feels like home.

The day we moved in, things were a little different. We opened the door and the house appeared bigger than we'd remembered it. Bob dashed straight between our legs, into the bedroom, and promptly pissed on the floor (he must have smelt the dogs that used to live there). Without any furniture, the cottage was a little echo-y, and we tiptoed around as if we were intruders. Laura, the demon decorator, thought she'd have the whole house repainted in about a week! Just as soon as the thousands of webs and their creators were dealt with. Out in the garden and the surrounding paddocks it was another matter. The previous owners had left for their new home about three months before, and it was mid-October before we picked up the keys. Mid-October is late spring, and spring in the sub-tropics is when nature really shows off. Grass grows while you watch and what had once been a vegetable garden now looked like an impenetrable thicket. We wandered around the property, and eventually summoned up the courage to voice a bit of negativity. “What the fuck have we done?” may not be the actual words, but they certainly convey the spirit of the matter. It seemed like someone had dropped us in some “Good Life” set and said:

“You play Tom, you're Barbara, now get on with it.”

(For those readers too young to know what I'm rabbiting on about, Google it. If this book survives long enough, I wonder if Google it will mean anything in years to come...)

We were so caught up in the rush of excitement and planning, that we had forgotten that not everything has to be done now, or even better, yesterday. The habit of living on a knife-edge had become so ingrained into our first reactions to the new home that it took us a few hours to realise that there was no need to rush, no need to panic. We were home, and if the veggie patch didn't look like the ones in our dreams and my favourite books, we could do some more work on it and gradually, it would take shape. At last, we weren't going anywhere! There was, of course, plenty to be done, and some of it couldn't wait.

As I mentioned, Laura has a thing for decorating, and can't wait to see results. I absolutely agree with this attitude, ideally, as long as I don't actually have to do any of the work myself. I did attempt to help, and the results are still there to see; any wall that looks as if it's still waiting to be finished, that's my handiwork. However, my complete lack of DIY skills, honed from years of incompetence in Glasgow and before, seemed to be starting to change. Perhaps it's that we had some expert advice and help, and perhaps it's that New Zealanders still pride themselves on their practicality and initiative but, by the time we came to putting in a new window, a feat so exciting that it gets it's own little chapter, I felt nearly competent!

Some changes we had planned were outside the realm of DIY. We had promised ourselves much more outside living space than the cottage originally had. Finding a builder in the area looked like it was going to be very difficult. The town of Kerikeri is growing at such a rate that any good builders were either up to their neck in ongoing projects, or had seen a chance and set up construction companies to pay lesser builders to do their bidding. It seemed to be sewn up tight. So we considered ourselves very lucky when we saw a small ad in the paper: "Local builder returned from overseas. No job too small or too big". I gave him a call, and he sounded great, delighted that the advert hadn't been a waste and happy to come round and give us an estimate for the work. We had experienced nothing but trouble from builders in Scotland. We were probably just unlucky, but nothing seemed to go right; the cost was always double the estimate and the finished result ever-so-slightly crap. So when Pete came to meet us, we held out little optimism that this would work out well. On the other hand, the work needed to be done or we would get into summer with no useable outdoor area. Pete was an unusual man. Strong, wiry and invariably grinning, and with the smallest, whitest false teeth I'd ever seen (and I've seen a few) with a high-pitched giggle for his own bad jokes. We discussed the plan:

"You want a deck how deep?" he queried.

"Three metres would be ideal," we suggested.

"That's massive", he said, "if you want a verandah on that, it'll be one hell of a roof".

But I half-closed my eyes and imagined the deck with our long, thin dining table on it, benches either side, and suddenly, it was full of people, the table groaning with lunch, and the sound of conversation and laughter. Either I had just seen our future, or I'd hallucinated an advert for pasta sauce. I assumed it must be the former, so we insisted on the oversized deck, and Pete started drawing up plans.

"This is going to cost a fair bit" he worried on our behalf, perhaps concerned that we might change our minds. But he came up with a price and sheepishly presented it to us and, to his surprise and delight, we said yes! We had been so accustomed to the initial estimate being at least double our budget that we couldn't even bring ourselves to barter, so close to our guess was his price. He was used to much bigger projects than ours, so this was a relatively simple task, and within a few weeks we had a really big sheltered outdoor dining and living area.

But something wasn't right. The new addition looked wonderful, and very practical, but the house now looked brand new. We perused magazines, the internet, and we recalled the villas we'd seen as we drove north. Clearly the verandah required some cosmetic additions. Then we discovered that there's a company in Auckland who manufacture all the old decorative woodwork that so characterises these venerable houses, so down we drove to Auckland again! The range of decorative woodwork was immense and we decided, vacillated, decided again, fretted over fretwork and worried that we'd get the proportions all wrong. Then we closed our eyes and made a final decision. A few days later the pieces we'd ordered arrived, and the garage was cleared and became a temporary spray paint shop, whilst the intricate mouldings were readied for fitting. And, one evening after a day's work, I came home and behold! With the lacework and fretwork in position, a dramatic transformation had occurred. The house and its deep deck looked as if it had been there forever. Even the keenest eyed neighbours have been surprised to discover that these elements were not part of the original nineteenth century design. For the first time that I could remember, we'd had some building work completed that was actually better than we had envisaged, and without an argument with the builder! I'll tell you what, though, that lacework and fretwork takes ten times longer than the rest of the verandah to decorate! I'm not surprised that modern houses don't incorporate these lovely additions, it's nothing to do with the look, it's the work!

Meanwhile, the house itself was still a shell of our future home. On leaving Glasgow, all the possessions that we chose to bring to our new life had been packed into a shipping container. The expert at the removals company had assured us that everything we'd shown him would fit. He was so wrong and, with some regret and just the slightest possibility of raised voices, we reluctantly selected those things that were to go to our Glasgow friends or, in some cases, charity shops. And now this container was slowly steaming its way across the oceans, and a Christmas without furniture was rapidly approaching. Alex, the previous owner of the farm, had moved away from the area, but his parents lived nearby and became tremendous supporters of our new life. Emma and Phillip had moved to New Zealand about forty years ago, and in a similar way to us, had fallen in love with a property near the bay. They were amazingly posh! Emma was the uncrowned Queen of Kerikeri, personal friends with British royalty, a retired actress, with a stately and, until you got to know her, rather intimidating demeanour, and Phillip an ex-naval officer, forward-thinking political advisor, and slightly brow-beaten husband. But they were so lovely, not at all aloof, and could not have been more helpful when it came to their new project of equipping us with the essentials of life in Northland, and basically taking us under their experienced wings. From out of Emma and Phillip's barn came an old bed, an armchair or two, some kitchen furniture and countless bits and pieces that were to serve as our essentials until the container ship docked.

After what seemed like an age, just before Christmas, it arrived, and a telephone call from the shipping company gave us the good, and the bad news:

"Your container is in Auckland, isn't that good news?" we were breezily informed, "we should have your stuff up north with you on about the twenty eighth of December!"

"Is there any chance we could have it delivered before

Christmas?" we pleaded.

"I'm really sorry, I don't think that'll be possible, but I will ask."

We didn't hold out much hope; the shipping company seemed very busy, and I'm sure we weren't the only ones hoping to have their container immediately. But equally, I did not trust the post-Christmas delivery date. Traditionally, everything closes until well into the New Year and I suspected that the government officer from Biosecurity, whose job it is to oversee the unpacking of the container, wouldn't be flexible if he was meant to be on holiday. But a day later, the shipping company contacted us again:

"Your container should be with you on the twentieth of December!"

We mentally hugged the lovely lady.

"Thank you so much!" we gushed, and immediately contacted the Ministry of Agriculture and Fisheries officer to let him know when and where to come and see the container being unpacked.

At last the day arrived, and it was like Christmas had come, only five days early. Alan, the Ministry man, arrived before the container and he was delightfully down to earth:

"I've a list of the boxes I want to see, but don't worry, we're not trying to catch you out, just to make sure that there's nothing you are bringing with you that could cause an environmental disaster."

We had heard so many varying stories about the MAF men but this was the first time we had come across them ourselves. Not all the stories were positive; rumours abounded on internet forums (fora?) of confiscated heirlooms, garden tools being soaked in disinfectant and fines imposed. We looked through the list of forbidden items Alan had supplied, and could see nothing that might cause problems. At last, the container arrived, the huge truck skillfully negotiating the narrow drive in beeping reverse. And there, in the yard, were all the things without which we had felt slightly adrift. Three tireless and enthusiastic men appeared from the cab and set about distributing the boxes, all wrapped in identical wrappers. Fortunately, they had also been well labelled. Clearly, these guys had done this job more than once. What we didn't realize was that their remit was to unpack all the boxes too. We had assumed they would simply unload the container and then drive off, but no, they were ours for the day, and incredibly helpful. When we told them that most of the boxes were to be stacked in the old shearing shed as we had nowhere near the space in our tiny house to unpack everything, they were so delighted the job was a simple one that they offered not just to unpack, but to assemble any of the furniture that had arrived flat-packed.

And so it was that, over the course of the day, the

house became a home, furnished in a somewhat familiar style, to our excited gasps of:

"Look! Here's that painting I knew would go here!" And

"Wow! I'd completely forgotten we had this!"

Laura's biggest delight was the rediscovery of a set of floral mugs that she had missed for the months that they'd been at sea. Meanwhile, there was a tense moment in the garage that was the temporary depot for the boxes that needed to be inspected. A tent had been packed away, ages ago, without a good clean and the soil and grass that had accompanied its hasty packing up in a muddy field near Coniston in England was released into its new home in Northland. We looked on aghast as grass seed spilt onto the concrete floor. Alan merely murmured,

"Now that's the kind of thing we like to watch out for. Just make sure that it's all swept up and it'll be fine"

I was sure he was going to use that "fine" word in a totally different sense. And that was the only drama of the day. Actually there was one other drama, but so slight that I've nearly forgotten it. Everything that arrived had been wrapped and packed with almost obsessive care. Even single lightbulbs came triple wrapped and then boxed to ensure their safe delivery. Everything, that is, except our microwave oven, which, probably as an afterthought, had been wrapped in one layer of brown paper and, testament to a rough passage, was dented dramatically. The delivery men were incensed that the packers could have been so careless and insisted that we should put in a complaint. But we assured them that, since everything else was in good order and we knew that they hadn't mishandled anything, we really didn't mind. By evening it was complete. The men were waved away southward with a case of beer, their job very well done, and we just stood at the doorways of the tiny rooms and sighed happily. Everything was unpacked and looked so familiar and so out of context, but we were well nested. And very comfortable.

Gardening & Tree Planting

We used to live in the west end of Glasgow, and, whilst it was leafy and green, and the flat did have a small shared garden at the back, no way could we describe ourselves as gardeners. We had made a few attempts at planting the back garden but Bob, as a puppy, and the neighbours' young children were happier with lawn, and had inadvertently removed anything resembling a seedling. To the front of the house lay the river Kelvin, and beyond that, Glasgow's Botanic Gardens, so our need for green havens was satisfied without our input. Moving to a small farm of twenty two acres was a bit of a change of pace.

At first, we treated the existing garden as sacrosanct and were loath to remove, or even prune, the plants that were established. It seemed such a shame to destroy someone else's hard work. But five minutes later, we had got over that. The first revision started in the veggie garden, but the biggest change was the big lawn at the front to the house. No, let me be more precise, what we really had was a house in a paddock with the grazier's bulls in it. All that prevented the bulls from coming in to borrow a cup of sugar, or asking the way to the nearest china shop, was a single-strand electric fence. And this presented Bob with a problem. On the one hand, the bulls were intriguing. Big, slow moving, and smelling ever-so faintly of raw steak, he just had to take a closer look; but on the other, he discovered, for the first time, the devilish New Zealand invention that is the electric fence. All it took was one jolt - howling and in need of immediate compassion, he rushed to the front door and when we let him in, he hid under the bed for the rest of the morning. He may have grown up on the mean streets of Glasgow, but that didn't stop him being as wet as a great-aunt's kiss.

Of course, the bulls had to be banished to the other paddocks, and the electric fence dismantled. And then the grass grew. Almost as we watched, the Kikuyu sprouted, the weeds thrived, and the house started to disappear behind a rising tide of vegetation. We didn't know the answer to the question that now arose, which was how do you turn a paddock, bullshit and all, into a lovely lawn? But we had a thought. The grass was too lush and tall to think about taking a mower to it, but the tractor was sitting idle in the shed, and next to it was the "slasher"; well isn't that just a glorified lawnmower? It certainly looked like one, with its wide deck and single, evil-looking spinny bladey thing. So I suggested to Laura that we ask our grazier how to use the device, and planned to get the job done at the weekend. Then I came home from work and, much to my amazement, a friendly farmer must have come round and cut the paddock for hay. But no! Laura, in the true spirit of "how hard can it be?" had worked it all out, and, despite one or two little glitches (like pulling a wheelie in third gear), had the paddock tamed and, with half-closed eyes, the lawn was on its way. (And half-closed eyes were all I could muster as the hayfever had now kicked in...).

It didn't take us long to realise that using the tractor to mow the lawn was not the way forward. It might have the brute strength to turn an overgrown meadow into a garden, but it was too blunt an instrument to maintain it. So it was with much delight to me that we had to go and buy a ride-on mower. And despite her prowess with Billy (as the old Massey-Ferguson 135 was now named), Laura seemed nervous of an expensive, purpose-built mowing machine. But not for long. These days we vie for the chance to mow, and it gives us three hours of mindless, headphones-on cruising around the garden at a stately seven kilometres an hour.

However, a big, bare, two acre lawn with one enormous oak tree was not what we had in mind for our front garden, so next on the list was a bit of tree planting. I had in my mind's eye a shady woodland area, with decorative specimen trees, dappled shade, and beautiful lawn between. For reasons I can't explain, this is my personal idea of bliss. It just does it for me. So all we needed was a lot of trees. And a bit of hard work. And some vision of how things might look in, oh, twenty years of waiting. So off we went to the myriad of garden centres in Kerikeri to look at trees, get some advice, and start a forest. There were a lot of trees. And there was a lot of advice available, too. We took a few of the former, and a great deal of the latter, and then went home, with a trailer we'd borrowed from one of the garden centres, and I proceeded to dig. I have never dug so much in my life. Even if I had been a 1970s hipster in San Francisco I wouldn't have dug as much as this. But all of this digging came with an almost instant result. By late that afternoon we had a little area between the cottage and the main road laid out with little trees, none of them higher than two metres, but an embryonic leafy glade nonetheless.

There is something deeply therapeutic in the process of planting trees. It certainly helps that the deep, dark, loamy soil where we live is easy to dig into. To dig down, to see the worms, and smell the earth, strain the back, measure the hole for the root ball, getting the angle of the trunk just right, packing in the soil, and knowing that you've just started a young tree on the path to possible greatness many years hence, possibly long after your own lifetime, these things are very satisfying. Meanwhile, Laura was gradually developing enough confidence to start imposing her green fingers on the rest of the garden. In truth, she really is a gardener and, if she never really knew how to be one before we moved here, she clearly had an innate understanding of how a garden grows, what plants require in order to thrive and how to bring harmony to the natural entropy of an unruly flower bed. Also, she doesn't hate weeding like I do. So the garden was taking shape as we made small changes which gradually added up to big alterations. With every season, it became more of our garden and less of what we had inherited. Now we look out at the lawn, the trees, the flower beds and the vegetable garden, and we feel satisfied that this place may never be entirely ours, for how can you own a patch of dirt? But it looks as if we live here, we work here and we have temporarily, and for the next few years, made it our place.

Buying Another Car

Despite the one hundred percent pure image that clean, green, New Zealand encourages the world to have of it, it is also a nation of car owners and car lovers. When I first visited New Zealand, and especially the South Island, in the late 1980s, it was very reliant on the durability and easy maintenance of post-war British cars. Trade restrictions meant that imported cars from Japan were very expensive and the rolling stock was becoming a little tired. Twenty years on, I was a little surprised to discover, even before we arrived here, that now there is a massive glut of imported cars. However, when I saw the prices of them, my surprise dissolved. Competition is fierce and, if you know what you want to buy, you can even select it before it leaves Japan (or Singapore, or Hong Kong) and have it checked over.

Living in a rural area makes car owning a necessity. Public transport is very limited so if you can't drive you'd have to rely on the kindness of others. This explains why a fifteen year old can drive, but it doesn't explain why so many people drive like fifteen year olds. I have always been a big fan of the French notion of rural mobility, where teenagers are allowed little more than powered bicycles, but here, low slung, wide-bore-exhausted, noisy Japanese machines are the preferred transport. As I've already described, when we first encountered the typical national habit of junction impatience as practiced by many New Zealanders, we developed a theory that, behind the wheel of a car, the relaxed attitude to life's frustrations could be vented in a gentle Dr Jekyll manner. Now we're just used to it and, if tailgated, we merely slow down and allow the aggressive Mr Hyde to pass (usually to discover that they want to drive no faster than we were anyway). We always assume that, if a car is waiting at a junction, it will pull out, but only once we have approached close enough to necessitate seriously hard braking. It's just an expression of a different way of doing things, and not really upsetting enough to whinge about!

Since we live on a small farm where mud and gravel or dirt roads are often under our wheels, it made sense to buy a four wheel drive car, perhaps the kind of car that is so popular on the English urban school run, but we would buy it to use as the manufacturer intended rather than for its intimidating properties. We took a trip to Whangarei and called in at a used-car dealer. We had already bought a Jeep in Auckland when we first arrived, so I had some idea of what to expect from the dealer but, after years of buying cars in Britain, where an unwitting punter in a used car sales yard can sometimes feel like a newborn lamb surrounded by a pack of friendly wolves that may smile but will still rip you to shreds, I was still taken by surprise. Here, the salesman was not only very approachable, but he applied no pressure. If we hadn't previously experienced the same relaxed attitude, I'd have been amazed and a little suspicious. We had a look around, we asked a few questions and we test drove a car or two. Having chosen a very well looked after estate car that was about ten years old, we sat down with the sales people and worked out how we were going to buy the car, bearing in mind we had only recently arrived and our money was still taking its own sweet time to catch us up. So we explained this to Darren and he said:

"As soon as we've sorted the rego, take the car home with you and we'll get the money off you when it arrives in your bank".

We appeared a little surprised by this, I think because, coming from the UK, where trust has become a little scarce and driving off in a used car without paying for would be too much of a temptation to some people, here it would never be considered by even the hardest used car salesman.

"Aren't you worried that we might just disappear and not pay?" we asked.

"Yeah, right!" said Darren, "where are you going to go?"

He had a fair point. We could drive as far as the south of the South Island, and then what? We'd certainly get caught sooner or later, and that went some way to explaining his laconic attitude. However, it was also a good reminder of the refreshing view of life that exists here. Why would you behave like a criminal if you didn't have to? In some parts of the world, trust has become whittled away to the point that we vaguely remember what it was with nostalgia, like an old gramophone, useful at the time but no place for it now. The intangible quality that comes with trust as part of the national psyche is priceless.

Our Friends

When we decided to move to New Zealand, I thought, at times, about what Alain De Botton, the Swiss philosopher/ writer, (Google him, he's a fascinating author) says about The Art of Travel, and particularly about how, when we travel to distant and wonderful destinations, we often forget that we bring ourselves on the journey. That is to say, if we suffer asthma at home, we will probably suffer it on holiday too. If we leave home with a headache, we may well arrive with one. And if we didn't like ice cream when we departed, it's unlikely that we will suddenly have developed a taste for it on arrival. Our destination will only be as good to us as our moods and tastes dictate. This omission of ourselves when we imagine a new life abroad is quite crucial. For me, the most important feature of our unknown journey to the antipodes had been the people we would meet, befriend and spend time with. A beautiful destination may be an empty delight without the support, sharing and most importantly, the communal eating and drinking that defines good friendship.

Of course, as a couple, we have each other, and it certainly helps that we are best friends, as well as soul-mates (much as I'd love to think of a better term!). For a holiday we are a self-sufficient unit, one little cocoon of cosy smugness. However, for the purposes of a new life, stretching into weeks, then years, a circle of good friends is vital. Not knowing a place makes me a social sponge, and I have noticed as I age, that I have a tendency to allow my notions of a place to be modified by the attitudes and opinions of the friends I make there.

It is no accident, then, that both Laura and I have a deep love of this part of New Zealand, as the first friends we made here were Wayne and Millie. Initially I wondered whether they were just very hospitable people, and would be the same for any strangers who need some point of reference, but now we have known them for years I know that our friendship is deeper than that. And because we know them as well as we do, we are incapable of describing them. I should have made some notes when we first met, but that would have seemed calculating, and I'm no journalist. They are beautiful people; naturally, everybody with a good heart emanates beauty. But they are quite unusual too. I have never encountered such power houses of activity. When we first met them, they had just opened a new dental practice. Eighteen months later, they had sold it, moved and decorated a massive old villa on a stunning block of land (this story will be recounted later), landscaped it, built a road to it, planted a vegetable garden and terraces for olives and citrus trees, planted a vineyard, and had another baby, their first son, (and much to my intense pride, my godson).

Most people I know talk about their dreams, some of them, over a lifetime, work towards their goals and achieve them. Wayne and Millie describe their dreams, and then, by then end of the week, have found some way of fulfilling them. And, before you ask, these are not rich people. They are very resourceful, financially courageous and they get up at half past five in the morning. As I write this they are sailing around the world on a yacht just big enough for all six of them. Bon Voyage!

The first person that Millie had introduced me to was a doctor who worked in the medical centre where their original dental practice was. Harriet had just nipped into the waiting room to ask Millie if they were going out on their boat at the weekend. I said

"Hello!", and, busy person that she is, Harriet just "hello!"'d back before disappearing back to work. A couple of weeks later, it was as if we'd known Harriet (or Harri as she prefers to be known) and Guy, her husband, all our lives. Everyone must be familiar with the feeling when you fall into a friendship, when you can't remember a time when you didn't know your friends. Guy and Harri are in that category for us - people without whom the level of our enjoyment of life here would be unimaginable. Harri is the down to earth half of their partnership, pretty, wise, pragmatic, hardworking, and very funny, she is the breadwinner and anchor for the two of them, whilst Guy, (with whom I have a 'bromance' so I'd better watch what I say) is the dreamer and schemer. Apart from being a skilled ironer, and general househusband, he is the networker and social entertainment expert. Bearded and rascally, with a passion for good wine, he is a handsome man cast in the guise of a 1950s rogue in the Terry Thomas or David Niven mould. They settled here a little before we did, having spent a year travelling around New Zealand, Harriet doing locum work in various medical practices, Guy becoming the well-known man about town wherever they went. Of all the places they visited, the one they liked the most was Kerikeri, and thus, and knowing them as well as we do, they provided us with a very cheap shortcut to feeling good about our choice of home. Sure, we can't wait to travel around these islands, but we are happy we placed the pin in the map as we did. And without them, we may have looked elsewhere. Who knows how much of this is luck or fate? I'm just happy that it worked out this way.

Putting in a Window

Our little cottage, in typical Victorian fashion, is fairly dark, with a poor ratio of windows to rooms. Whilst we were getting the deck and veranda added to the outside of the house to give us some much-needed outdoor living space, we had a window in the kitchen removed and replaced with big French doors. Not only did this give us much more daylight in the kitchen and access to the garden, it also left us with a lovely big spare sash window casement. Pete, the builder, suggested he put it back into the wall in the living room for additional light, but we were starting to grow weary of his constant presence. Perhaps it was the giggling. We also noticed that builders take so much longer when you pay them by the hour, as opposed to paying them by the job. Then our friends Wayne and Millie suggested to us that it might be a task we could tackle ourselves. It may need repeating that I am not a DIY expert. I am in awe of anyone who can measure twice, cut once (I'd end up doing the opposite), and then not regret the whole damn thing and reach for the yellow pages. If you need a tooth, or a whole mouth rebuilt, I'm your man, but hand me a drill 100 times the size and I'm an embarrassment to the species. Despite my reluctance to be party to anything that involved cutting a large hole in the side of our new home, Wayne was very persuasive, mainly because he is brilliant at home maintenance, and not only that, he loves it!

Casting my misgivings aside, we thought it might be fun to discover how to do something as real, macho and, let's face it, useful, as adding a new window. By the time the appointed day arrived, I was very nervous about the whole thing. I had visions of us getting halfway through the job before discovering that the hole was too big, or the window was unsuitable, or something unthinkable that would make completing the project impossible and then finding that the solution would take weeks to fix. This is called pessimism, and is the refuge of the unconfident and the inept. (After all, the glass can be as empty as it damn well likes if you know how to refill it).

Wayne and Millie arrived early with a slew of important looking tools, and our friends Guy and Harri arrived shortly afterwards. Apparently, all our friends were here to help, not just to lend enthusiasm to the project. We measured the frame, we measured the wall, we took a serious sounding circular saw and, oh my sweet lord! we cut a hole in our lovely living room wall. The kauri wood smelled sweet and clean, amazing since it was last hewn a hundred years ago, and the hole, dusty though it was, looked about the right sort of size. By lunchtime things were starting to look pretty workmanlike. I had discovered phrases like "offer it up" and "make good". Furthermore I could wear a joiner's holster belt with the appropriate swagger. Once the frame was in place, the wine started to flow. By mid-afternoon, we were nearly complete and nearly drunk.

And there it is. I'm sitting just next to it. It opens and closes just like a real window, it looks like it was there from the start and, much more importantly, it's our window, a piece of physical work that I could never even have contemplated in the soft consumerist funk that surrounded my life in Glasgow. It's only a window, I do know that but, do you remember the barn raising in Witness, a Harrison Ford film from the eighties? That window is our barn raising, our moment when we realised that our life had changed and that, with the help and enthusiasm of our new friends, we could step outside our normal level of comfort and enjoy doing things we'd never done before. I think I'll make a brass plaque for it! Oh, and the bedroom needs a French door onto the new deck. I'm not even nervous of it now.

Out and About on the Water

The Bay of Islands has the second bluest skies in the world. It's official. A climatologist measured them. Of course, he might have just been on holiday here and wanted to make it tax-deductible... but, from the water, on a sunny day, it's hard to disagree with the scientist's findings. The sky is blue as a bastard. The sea is even less legitimate. And with safe, protected waters, plenty of accessible boat ramps and a glut of reasonably priced small motor boats, it would be churlish not to get out on the water. Laura is an experienced diver who in the past had immersed herself in the cold waters around Scotland, apparently for fun, so for her the South Pacific, which drops to a perishing sixteen degrees in the winter, is absurdly warm.

The bay isn't exactly a desert, either. Scallops abound and, whilst scuba diving for them is no more fun than picking field mushrooms, no one refused natures bounty because it wasn't pretty enough. Besides, the saltwater crayfish is also plentiful here and they are, in my opinion, even better fare than lobsters (and they have no snappy claws, although they do have spiny spines). Our diving, before we came here, was mainly for the amazing sights of the sub-aquatic realm. We had never taken seafood home with us, but here the emphasis is different. Certainly, there are some wonderful vistas to be seen. Indeed, the amazing Jacques Cousteau proclaimed the Poor Knights Islands one of the top five dive sites in the world, but New Zealanders feast on food as well as views, and if the food is free, then why wouldn't they? So off we go, harvesting scallops from the sandy shallows of the bay and daring to grab crayfish from their rocky holes (and trusting that we're not just thrusting our mitts into the maw of a Moray!).

There are hundreds of little occasions when we have cause to turn to each other and wonder if we ever thought our life would include this; diving for our food is one of them that really shines. That it's from the back of a little fibreglass boat that sits in our garage on its trailer when not in use doesn't hurt, either. One of the assumptions I had held about people who spend time on the water was that they were not like me. Either they were fishermen, in which case they had one of the most risky occupations ever devised, or they were yachties and involved in one of the most haughty occupations ever devised. It turns out I was wrong. Here all types of people get out on the water. They might be there just for fun or on jet skis (which I still find intensely irritating), but they are more likely to be catching their supper in anything from a tiny "tinny", which is an aluminium-hulled boat built for strength and longevity, inflatable sided plastic-hulled boats called a

RIBs, beloved of the military, the coastguard, and anyone who can afford them, or in beautiful yachts that may well have sailed a family across the pacific to a new home. But what it is, is egalitarian. No one looks up or down on their fellow boatmen. And, despite what I expected, there's none of the swagger or showiness amongst the waterborne. Or if there is, I'm mercifully oblivious to it.

Our friends (and my first employers) Wayne and Millie came here by yacht. That they had sailed, with their young daughter, across the ocean to be here suggests to me that there are few undertakings that would cause them much stress. We have been very fortunate that they introduced us to this part of the world. Their love of the way of life that we have now embraced has been a real breath of sea air. I suspect that we might have been reluctant to stop lubbing the land so much if it wasn't for the enthusiasm with which they dragged us into the water! You can scoot across the bay in about forty minutes with a powerful enough craft, and they do have a powerful enough craft. It didn't take much more than a day out on the boat, diving, swimming and just bedazzled by the water's glint before we were hooked. We saw dolphins, fairy penguins, even orcas, and we feasted on the freshest of fresh seafood.

A year on from our first forays into boating, we began to watch the weather forecasts with a very different eye. There's weather suitable for gardening, and there are days that are good only for the plants, when we have to retreat indoors and pretend that this isn't paradise; but the best, the most memorable days involve the water. The boat and gear is almost always ready and the fuel tank almost always full. The trailer is hitched up and a suitable boat ramp is chosen. Then there's the task of launching. Thankfully, reversing the boat and trailer down the slip soon became reasonably easy and now I can do this without completely embarrassing myself (it wasn't always so). Once the boat's in the water and the car parked, all the land-locked cares vanish. The boat bounces over the waves, in a way that makes me feel nervous and happy and, whether the destination is a fishing spot, a visit to some friends, a dive, or even a secluded, inaccessible restaurant (honest, there is one!) the joy of being there is profound. I'll never criticise yachties again!

More Aquatic Tales

New Zealanders, I am led to believe by statistics that I just made up, are the most boat-owning nation in the world. I suppose it might even be true. All the settlers who created modern Aotearoa were seafarers. From the Maori migrants of Polynesia, to their European cousins years later, they all came here by boat. There's brine in the blood of most New Zealanders I have met, and that sea, so overfished in many parts of the world, continues to reward people here with its abundance.

Guy and Harri have recently become the proud parents of a five metre RIB and, despite some childhood illnesses, their baby goes well. Named "Rubber Duck" it's sleek and over-powered. We slalomed to our fishing spot, due to a bizarre steering anomaly. Then dropping our anchor, we cast our rods and bobbed on a soporific swell. We sipped bottled water, and wondered why we had all forgotten to bring beer. It didn't take long for a fish to feel sorry for our lack of refreshing ale. They certainly didn't seem to care about our appalling technique. Laura, who's never caught a fish of any sort, was their first victim. She played this generous aquatic sacrifice like a squealing teenager, eventually handing the rod to Guy to land the suicidal snapper. The fish was probably relieved to pass into the next realm, and calm was restored.

The Pigfish Laura subsequently hooked obviously hated calm. Exposed to even more shrieking than the snapper, it may have been the ultrasound that stunned it. We were assured by some laughing fishermen a few metres away that it would be delicious. Still troubled by faulty steering, we snaked our way to a rocky outcrop known for its excellent green-lipped mussels. Harri donned mask, snorkel and gloves and proceeded to catch our entree. Like a competitor from "Jeux sans Frontières", she rose and fell on the briny swell and caught almost enough for a Mormon family reunion.

It's a relaxing way of spending an afternoon, this boating thing, and well worth the hassle of launching and retrieving the boat. In the process it gives us a splendid appetite. And a thirst. By happy coincidence, there was plenty of beer back home in the fridge. So, with the boat on its trailer again, and drink in hand, we inspected our catch. Two fish, both good sized, and about thirty large mussels. In the kitchen, Harri and I gutted the fish, removed the scales, and realised why most fishing boats have a little table at the stern. Scaling creates a piscine blizzard but, instead of melting, they leave a pungent, fishy fingernail of such transparency that they easily become lost. Until, days later, the scale ripens and the nose locates what the eye had missed. In the last of the daylight, the fish were prepared, the table and the sun set, the barbecue lit and the side dishes magicked into existence. The fish were grilled to perfection, but then Laura noticed that she was being watched. By a dead fish. Covering its eyes did nothing to restore her appetite. It seems that Pigfish are only good eating if you have acquired a taste for cotton wool mixed with pin-sharp bones. We may never do so. Snapper, of course, is one of the best tasting food in the world, and freshly caught by our own incompetence makes it doubly delicious.

Perhaps I'm alone in this and, heaven knows, taste really is a matter of - um- taste, but I really don't understand the culinary sensation that is the Pacific mussel. Most New Zealanders are fiercely proud of them and certainly they are lovely to behold. They look like huge, green-edged versions of the cold water mussels we were used to in Europe and I'm sure that, as filter feeders, they are far cleaner than their European cousins. But they seem to retain their beard with a tenacity that makes eating one as pleasant as seasoning seafood with a wee hank of pubic hair. Then there's the determined elastic band that is impervious to the hundred or so pounds per square inch that the teeth can exert. They taste really good, but I don't like having to argue with my food. Please don't call me a whingeing pom (I've just discovered that it's now become a politically incorrect term, so if you do, I could have you imprisoned). Instead, if there is a way of consuming these beautiful, huge molluscs without a fight, please come and cook some for me and I will be your friend for life. I want to love everything about our new home and, so far, the mussel isn't coming to the party.

But please can I have some more Snapper?

The Seasons

It's now April, and therefore, the start of autumn. I still have some small problem with the seasons. I can understand the logic of it, but I can't quite get my head round the upsidedownedness of it all. April just doesn't sound like autumn to me. We do have April showers, though! Last Thursday the rain, which had been steady for a couple of days, suddenly turned dramatic. This is something that, in Britain I'd only experienced in a thunderstorm. The sky went dark, the rain became torrential and outside was a soaking, forbidding nightscape, best left to melancholy film noir sets. But here the scene is set in the sub-tropics and makes a British squall seem positively amateur. The sky went black, not black like night but that para-natural darkness of a solar eclipse, the rain drummed on the roof and, moment by moment, instead of the familiar gradual relenting of the pace, the power of the storm just increased. The water eventually had no more places to drain away, and everything that could carry it became a torrent. Streams matured into rivers, pasture became lakes and waterfalls started to look like world class cataracts. And then the rain really started. By the evening, the weather had become newsworthy and the local climate had achieved its fifteen minutes of fame. Phrases like "three months worth of rain in two days" and "the worst weather for a hundred and fifty years" were being passed around like "top trumps" attributes, and stories of people being marooned in cars, children having to stay at schools overnight and worse still, homes and houses being lost in landslips had become public knowledge. In the end, four hundred millimetres of rain fell in forty eight hours. Nobody was badly hurt and, in an act typical of the region, Friday dawned clear, bright and warm, as if completely ignorant of its predecessor's shocking behaviour.

In truth, everyone who was not badly affected by the storm must have had some grudging appreciation of its grandeur. It was big. I thought it was brilliant. I'm usually elsewhere when dramatic weather happens so it was good to be right in the middle of it! Even driving to work and seeing the roof of a car that had been abandoned the night before in a ditch and which was now just visible at the waterline made this a memorable event. Perhaps it's the effects of climate change, or perhaps it's just that our lives are so small in comparison with the moods of nature, but only three months after the "150 year storm" we had another one of almost equal severity. In fact, the effect of this one was more devastating as the ground, by mid-winter, was saturated with water and it runneth over - all over the bloody place. By then, of course, we were getting used to it.

So this is the vaguely unsettling aspect of a life here. The seasons are six months out of sync with my instincts. It almost seems that there should be other names for the months that apply more appropriately than the ones I have become accustomed to. I'm sure that this will become normal in time, but I do love the oddness of them. The climate too, is beguiling. It's at its best when not trying too hard. Summer is always at odds with itself as the heat comes with humidity. Northland isn't very good at hot weather, going from lovely and warm and breezy to hot and sultry, with little in between. The autumn and spring bring plenty of sunshine and, often enough, plenty of heat but as a reminder of the winter, the nights become chilly and clear. And the winter can seem damp and cold, a time for social hibernation, only to surprise us occasionally with a few days of balmy sunshine. How clichéd of me, an Englishman, to devote so much time to the weather but since our life is outdoors almost every day, it's hardly surprising.

Although I never intended or expected it to turn out this way, we have become farmers by default (because we have a tiny farm) and as a result, weather dependent (or obsessed). I have never met a farmer whose first topic of conversation was not the recent weather, and it's very hard for them not to sound like the eternal pessimist: if it's been raining heavily "the ground is all pugged up and we'll be losing half our feed", or if it's turned dry "the ground's really dried out, I don't know if we'll need to buy in some feed if this goes on". I don't suppose it's possible to be involved with farming for these issues to be far away, but it also seems to explain why the happiest farmers are the ones who are the most phlegmatic about the seasonal changes.

The really startling discovery though, is the sky. The first time I looked up on a clear night here I nearly fell over. The sky is vertiginous. It's bigger than you see it in urban Britain, and there's almost no light pollution, so it isn't just wide, it's deep, too. The constellations are mainly unfamiliar. Orion makes an appearance, and the Milky Way arcs across the canopy as it does in Scotland, but there are innumerable new stars to be seen and new patterns to become familiar with. At twilight, the International Space Station and other satellites race across the darkening sky, studiously ignoring us staring up at them (...or are they?). When the moon is full, its intense silver light casts shadows and illuminates so strongly that the dogs can race across the paddock after a ball without hesitation.

That the landscape is similar enough to Britain to seem comfortable, and the sky is the same sky, but that everything has been twisted into a new perspective, made new and interesting, and not just as a novelty, this is what grabs my attention so vigorously and with such delight. The climate is more extreme towards the warm end of the scale, more giving and forgiving, but also more dramatic. I can really understand why so many people from overseas have settled here, and how it has provided a home that is both comfortable and unpredictable in one breath.

Christmas in New Zealand

It takes a little time to become accustomed to a Christmas in midsummer. The clichés of snow, firelight, holly and mistletoe are so deeply ingrained in the subconscious of us northerners that even some of those New Zealanders who were born here, but whose ancestors migrated from Europe and America, miss those features of Christmas. So the midwinter stereotypes still persist, and the spray-on snow garnishing the window frames of shops looks very odd in midsummer! There are, of course some traditions of Christmas in New Zealand that have developed to be appropriate for the holiday.

It's traditional here for long summer weeks at the beach, and this is the time of year where the bach comes into its own (even if many of the traditional baches have long ago been replaced with seaside palaces of steel and glass). Families would go, year after year to their own little spot of beach, they would know all their neighbours, their families would grow up together, eat, party and play together, and strong communal ties would develop centered around a (somewhat rose-tinted) memory of endless sunny days. Of course, with the rough-hewn, often homemade and simple baches being replaced by the luxurious modern beach houses, and the cause-and-effect spiral of prices that accompanies this change, the tradition is dying. There is no doubt that, for many New Zealanders, this is a shame. The beach has started to become a symbol of wealth and privilege, and the traditional family bach is more likely to be part of an investment portfolio than a family campsite. I don't suppose there is a simple way of reversing this trend when there are more and more people and nobody is making new beaches. It doesn't stop us, as newcomers to these beautiful lands, attempting to recreate the nostalgic tradition.

Wayne and Millie have built a tiny beach hut, with a space flat enough for a tent or two and, for a crowd of us, the unspoken invitees, there's a magnetic draw to the seaside for a delicious Christmas feast from the barbecue, pizza oven and salad bowl. The wine flows, the pohutukawa glows crimson, and the night descends very slowly and very late. We revel in the midsummer warmth (OK, it does rain sometimes), we over eat and drink as if we really are about to hibernate, and we look forward to the months of February and March when the weather becomes really reliably summery, the boats are more often on the bay than not, and houses are only for sleeping in.

Being designated driver on Christmas day is a hardship to be borne with dignity. The day starts early as the sun rises at about five o'clock and, for us, breakfast is some kind of sparkling wine mixed with our own orange juice.

As our house guests awaken, bacon sandwiches appear in an attempt to prevent an early morning hangover. By mid morning, it's time for coffee and a walk around the paddocks with the dogs to greet the donkeys, bestow Christmas treats on them (bread rather than carrots is their preferred treat) and down to the stream for a round of enthusiastic dog-and-stick action. Suitably soaked and exercised, it's back to the house for the opening of presents and a late lunch, which will often be a hybrid of the traditional (roast potatoes and other veggies), the antipodean (barbecued scallops, crayfish and other seafood) and the modern (panna cotta, anyone?) Often, in addition, there's a roast ham there for the slicing on Christmas day and for many days to come. Mmm!

The wines of New Zealand are amazing. Classy Sauvignon Blancs and complex Pinot Noirs dominate, but there is a growing, high class viticulture here that is great and becoming greater. Christmas lunch only benefits from this, and the designated driver's nobility becomes legendary, because we're off to the beach as the afternoon wears on. A bonfire is built, more wine is drunk; the quality might well be diminishing, but we're beyond caring now, relining our stomachs with delicacies from the pizza oven, the barbecue, and the fridge. The sun starts to set, the fire is lit, the shadows and stories lengthen and the stars start to come out. The evening's glow slowly fades and as this lovely sun sets here, and as we snooze and chat contentedly under our soft velvety canopy of stars, with the lapping tide and crackling fire our background music, we remember that the same sun is rising on a cold and frozen Christmas morning in northern parts of the world.

It may take a while before we think of Christmas as a time for outdoors, al fresco food and short nights, but it doesn't take long to appreciate the delights of this time of year.

Perpetual Holiday

Since we first arrived in this lovely place and with enthusiastic regularity thereafter, one of the most commonplace questions we've been asked by New Zealanders was and is how we like their country. If we'd been having a really depressing time, this would have been a difficult question to answer, for all the locals that we've met have a fierce loyalty to the land, not at all a jingoistic nationalism but rather a pride in the wonderful place that so many have chosen as home or been fortunate to grow up in.

It's funny to think that, as newcomers to New Zealand we are still (and yes, I am counting the Maori and their ancestors) early settlers to this place, the most recently inhabited country on Earth. If a generation is about thirty-two years (that's the genealogical definition), then, at the most, only twenty-five generations of humans have walked these shores. And only the last six or seven generations have included the Pakeha colonials (that's the non-Maori migrants). No wonder we're still making it up as we go along.

But I digress!

"How do you like New Zealand?"

The question was asked and I haven't been polite

enough to answer it. Obviously, we like the place a great deal, and even after we had been here for many months, we still felt, as the sun warmed our backs in the garden, or the wine tickled our hearts at suppertime, that we were living on a perpetual holiday. Our choices of activity were holiday choices - should we take the boat out into the bay? Should we meet for a picnic at the beach? Or should we just lie in the hammock and enjoy a book? Unlike a shorter holiday, other choices might occur to us such as planting a veggie garden, or building a shed. But the atmosphere, the tone of living, to us was that of a long relaxing vacation, interspersed as infrequently as possible by the work which is constantly required to keep it all going. Even writing this book (I know, despite appearances, it took me a fair bit of time) would be almost unthinkable in my northern life, where the pace of events seemed to rob us of any time for reflection.

Then another winter happened. We had returned from a blissful trip to the South Island (which will be mentioned again later) in early June, to a Northland beset by driving rain. This was not the deluge I described earlier, and it never caused terrifying flooding and landslips but, in its way, it was just as pernicious. The rain was heavy enough to keep us indoors most of the time, and was occasionally heavy enough to come with power cuts, but the real heaviness was the effect that it had on everyone around including ourselves. For three months, there were only two days without rain. There were four subtropical cyclones that blew onto us and several more storms that were almost as bad but not graced with a meteorological title By the end of winter any trees, buildings and people that were vulnerable to them were bowed down or broken. Wisely, and by chance, most of our friends were away for much of the time, and whilst this was a good thing for them, it left us with a sense of social isolation that I like to think of as hibernation (because it sounds so much better than "depressed antisocial git"). Then, one morning, I was sitting on the deck, scratching the back of Bob's head and getting the occasional and rather biased, admiring ear-licks from Brodie, who as you will shortly discover, is Bob's younger brother. The sun was shining as it had been all weekend and, suddenly, it was all over, and the spell was broken. It wasn't that I was aware that winter had blocked out that holiday feeling, so much that I noticed the return of the sensation of the sun on my back. That our friends returned home just as the weather took a turn into spring helped a great deal, but I was a little jealous that they had escaped the winter and left us to experience a season of cabin fever on our own. We never migrated here for the weather, although it did feature in our choice of places to live, but I was surprised just how much the winter affected our psyche. Many of my patients and work colleagues attested that it had been an unusual winter, when the barometric depressions seemed to aggravate the emotional ones.

It's good to be back on perpetual holiday. There's nothing more effective than contrast when it comes to reminding us of our good fortune.

A Little Snack . . .

The attempt by the weather to ensure that we forget the deep blue and bright yellow of summer is best countered by creating some rituals designed to banish any negative feelings.

For a group of us, this is accomplished by the preparation, and more importantly, the consumption of comfort food. And so, with our good friends Guy and Harri, the 'Soup and Sandwiches' Sunday night was born. From humble beginnings, this has developed into a gentle competition for the most outlandish and exotic combinations palatable. We now know why pea and ham were first put together*, how to avoid the intense flatulence that Jerusalem Artichokes bring with them** (despite making the most delicious soup), and the preparation of a good stock has become an art form as well as a rewarding means of recycling. Sunday in the winter has now become a night to look forward to, the sky darkens early, the wind and rain can do what they like, the crackling of a wood fire beckons and the anticipation of a well-filled stomach, a good glass of wine and excellent company and conversation is only a short drive away.

* They're delicious. The saltiness of the ham balances

the bland creaminess of the pea. You knew that. It wasn't a secret.

** Asafoetida. Despite its awful smell in the raw, this spice renders the enzyme that produces climate-changing volumes of intestinal gas harmless. And Asafoetida loses its toxic smell once cooked.

Forget hibernation, this is what winters were made for. We alternate these events from one house to the other.

"It's our turn for the soup and sandwiches; you're in for a real treat this time!" I brag, "I'm doing a Chinese theme, hot and sour soup, with crispy duck rolls!"

"That's sounds good, but we've already raised the bar very high with the broccoli and Stilton soup and the bacon and avocado sandwiches!" comes back the equal boast.

And on it goes; we try to outdo each other, but we all end up winning. And so that I can invite you, humble reader (if you are indeed humble, and I have no idea why you should be) to take part in our Sunday extravaganza, I have included a couple of favourite recipes at this point. All you need to do is to choose a suitable evening, preferably a wintery one, light the fire and some candles, ensure you are with the very best of friends and prepare something along these lines:

Pumpkin soup and Chicken baguette:

Roast a whole chicken. If you carefully put some salted lemon-zesty butter under the skin and salt and pepper on the outside of the skin before you roast it, this will give you lovely, crispy crackling.

30 min before the chicken is done, surround it by some chunks of fresh pumpkin or butternut squash. Baste them with the juices from the chicken.

Once the bird is cooked, and the flesh is almost falling off the bone, tear (not cut) the best meat from the bird to furnish your sandwiches. Use whatever meat you prefer (unless you want to punish yourself).

Keep the chicken meat somewhere warm and covered.

Place the carcass in a large pan with a coarsely chopped onion, four big sticks of celery, a couple of chopped carrots and three bay leaves.

Cover with water and simmer for about an hour. Then strain the liquid into a smaller pan and taste. If it's a sweet and tasty stock, that's great. If it's a bit watery, reduce at a roiling boil until it is sweet and tasty. You should end up with about a litre.

Place the now softened celery, carrot onion and roasted pumpkin into the stock, add a little dry sherry, simmer for a few minutes to get the alcohol and associated bitterness away, then blend with a stick blender until smooth and velvety.

Season to taste, and add a little cream, soured cream or creme fraiche. And the soup is ready.

Take a baguette, cut it into longish sections and slice lengthways. Spread with butter and mayonnaise. Add a good handful of rocket leaves and plenty of the now cooling chicken. Season with salt and pepper. Grainy mustard is also good.

This is one of our favourites, and gives us loads of leftovers as well as a delicious meal.

Then there's Harri's tour de force (or is it tour de France?), and we always look forward to it.

French onion soup with separate cheese on toast sandwiches

Take 6 medium sized onions and chop them finely.

Fry slowly in a large pan with a teaspoon of brown sugar and a big knob of butter.

Cook slowly enough for them to soften, lose their water and finally caramelise without burning.

Add a couple of finely chopped garlic cloves and about a litre of beef stock (preferably homemade), and then a cup of white wine and half a cup of brandy Throw in a couple of bay leaves and some thyme.

Simmer covered for about 40min, then remove the bay leaves.

Meanwhile, take some slices of good fresh crusty bread (probably white) and drizzle with plenty of olive oil. Bake in a hot oven for a few minutes until the bread starts to dry out (but not brown yet).

Place some grated gruyere cheese on half the slices and place the other half of the slices on top and finely grate a mound of parmesan on top of the newly-formed sandwiches.

Put them back in the oven until the cheese is melted and the bread is toasted.

Serve the soup piping hot (nothing to do with being announced by pipers - it's the sound of something so hot that the steam that comes out of it is whistling, so I'm told) and dip those sandwiches in the soup! Mmm.

A few of years ago, another winter food tradition developed; the curry cook-off. It started innocuously enough;

"We're having a few friends round as a final supper before we move house" our friends Ann and Steve told us. "Bring a curry, anything you like, and if you have some Indian music on CD, could you bring that, too? We thought that, if enough people bring curries we could have a sort of competition!"

It was intriguing. I love cooking, and I love curries, and, being from the UK, I have an unreasonably high opinion of my ability to cook the best curry ever! It might not have happened yet, but I'm working on it. On the day, there was a great turn out, and ten different curries were tasted, enjoyed, tasted again and judged with little pieces of paper. There were all kinds of dishes; mild and creamy curries from the north of India, hot and sharp Goanese delights, and light and fragrant Thai offerings. I cooked as authentic a lamb chop Korma as I was able, taking the recipe from a book of traditional Indian food from the 1930s. The evening was a great success, and Frank, as overall winner with a delicious lamb and spinach dish, was awarded a tiny trophy, and allocated the task of hosting the next event. I came in second.

So how long does a tradition take to come into being? In this case, the next event, hosted by Frank and Sarah, sealed its fate as an annual occasion. On a hillside overlooking the sea, under a sheltering verandah, we gathered for the next feast. The curries were even more outlandish and spanned the entire breadth of Asia, from the middle east, right across to the Philippines. As last year's previous winner, Frank was excluded from the competition, but his curry was superb. This time I tried to win with a luxurious prawn biriyani, but Chris' delicate and delicious Thai green curry was a clear winner. I came in second.

The next year, we gathered at Chris and Amanda's house, and what a gathering it was, nearly fifty people and twenty curries. The table probably was actually groaning and the feast was an aromatic paradise. People we'd never met, friends of friends of friends, had heard about the event and joined in. Needless to say, the afternoon became evening before all of us, bellies full, got around to the judging. This time, Frank and I jointly took first place, I with an Indonesian beef rendang (my favourite curry of all) and Frank with a very complex layered rice dish with a wickedly hot and sour gravy. And so, with much tension, a tiebreaker was announced:

"You have to name all twenty ingredients in the Tom Yung Goong (Thai coconut chicken soup) that I've made" said Chris.

Frank and I went to it, thought and tasted, considered, and re-tasted. It was superb. It was complex, and damn, it, by one ingredient, I came in second.

As had become the tradition, the previous year's winner hosts the next event, and so we returned to Frank and Sarah's place for the fourth annual competition. I'll be biased and say that the standard was higher than ever, and with Frank out of the running for the prize, I was in a confident and competitive mood. I selected a curry that was a little left-field, an Indonesian hot and sour prawn recipe, and practiced and modified it until I thought it was delicious. It must have been appealing; even Laura, who has no tolerance for hot curries liked it. Once again, the curries spanned the whole of Asia and fed us like royalty, and it is with very little humility that I can now, at last, announce that I am the reigning curry champion!

Next year, we're the hosts!

House Moving

Our friends Wayne and Millie decided to move house. It's not so strange to discover that someone you know is moving house, and we weren't taken by surprise. They always seemed to be on the move from one place to the next, but they'd bought a very pretty parcel of land (section is the vernacular) by the sea and would move there as soon as they could.

One fine day in late spring, we packed ourselves into two cars and headed west. The reason became obvious eventually! Northland is really a peninsula and it wasn't long before we had crossed to the west coast. There's something strangely romantic and island-like about living on such a narrow spit of land. Now we faced the Tasman Sea, not the Pacific Ocean, and the coastline was very different; wilder, less populated and more exposed to the prevailing wind. The long, straight beaches were backed by dunes that extended for miles and rose, in some places, to hundreds of metres.

We headed south along the coast, through a few small towns that were just gearing up for the summer holiday season, when we noticed a knot of people on the beach looking out to sea. So, as you do, we decided to find out what the attraction was, and to our delight, we saw a pod of orcas swimming down the coast, only metres from the shore. I have never seen an orca except in films, and my excitement was akin to that of a child. This seems to be a common reaction to the close presence of cetaceans. I have no idea why they are singled out for such affection, but they are. It's irrational and, I suspect cultural, as there must be a fair number of Japanese and Faroe Islanders who have a more culinary leaning towards these beasts than we do. So off we went, following the orcas south. When we reached a town with a long jetty, we ran along it breathlessly and witnessed an almost holy moment when we could see the killer whales swim directly beneath our feet. Amazing!

By the time we reached Tane Mahuta we were almost ready for a disappointment, but instead, we were awestruck and delighted. Tane Mahuta is a tree. An old kauri tree. A big tree. That should probably read a BIG tree. The Department of Conservation has, rightly, made sure that no one can get too close because the attention would be too much for it, but even from a distance of fifty metres, it doesn't fail to impress. The "Father of the Forest" as it is known, is over two thousand years old, and looks like a pillar of some ancient cathedral built by giants. Coming near to it, even though we weren't the only visitors, there was an atmosphere of solemnity and everyone's voices hushed slightly. Laughing was right out of the question. There used to be millions of these behemoths, now there are hardly any left, which, bearing in mind the enthusiasm of our species for “free” timber is not surprising, but is rather tragic. We paid our respects, took our pictures and moved on.

Dargaville was the destination for the day. Dargaville is a farming town that used to be a logging town in the days when the kauri forest covered four million hectares. Now the primary reason for its existence is gone, and all that is left to show for it is a chocolate-brown mini-Mississippi of a river (the silt from the deforestation still clouds the water). It is a town that feels as if it’s waiting to wake from a coma, but is rarely visited, even by its close relatives, most of whom have given up hope that it will ever recover.

Appropriately, we had come here to look at a retirement home which was being retired. Built in the 1920s and, even more appropriately, made almost entirely from kauri wood, it was due for demolition to make way for something more modern, with lower ceilings, purpose-built ease of access for the infirm and, no doubt, a little less character. This house had character. It may have smelt a little of decay, but that couldn’t disguise the grandeur that was packed into the house when it was built as a family home all those years ago. Our friends were looking at this house from a perspective that was a little foreign to us. Was it right for them as a new home, and if so, could it be transported the one hundred and fifty kilometres to the Bay of Islands without destroying it? As a stranger to this notion of moving house, I was amazed. Is it really possible to just lift up a massive house, move it and set it down again without it falling to bits? Indeed it is, and it's a tribute to the ingenuity of New Zealanders, the building ability of their early settlers and the durability of the timber they used that this is a real prospect for many old houses once they outlive their use in their original location.

Having decided, changed their minds and then decided again that this was the house for them, Wayne and Millie handed over to the relocation experts and the house was on its way. The move itself is of such novel and mind-boggling ingenuity that it deserves a chapter to itself. So I've given it one. Our friends now have a house with a view, by the sea, and gradually, but remarkably quickly, it looks as if it was built there one hundred years ago. This grand old dame of a house, after years of little but slumber and sadness, now rings to the laughter (and tears) of family life.

From Dargaville we headed east once more, first to Whangarei where we hoped to find somewhere to eat as the the children were hungry. Just as we neared our home town, we decided to try one more place to eat, and ended up with one of those happenstances that can never be planned. Millie phoned from their car:

"There's a restaurant called The Sugar Boat that you just have to see!" came the message.

"We'll follow you!" I responded.

And so we took another diversion, off towards Waitangi, where the historic treaty was signed and, just on the water (but not floating) was an old schooner. In a former life she had been a sugar cane transport ship in Australia, then a small marine museum and now, finally, had come to rest near Paihia as a restaurant. We piped ourselves aboard and, just as the sun was setting, we sipped cocktails on the deck, toasting each other for our good timing. As darkness fell, we snuck below decks for a delightful meal and very rowdy conversation, mainly due to the abundance of children who had just spent hours in a car.

And so our friends had chosen their new house - toasts were drunk to the grand old lady of Dargaville, and the night turned into a celebration of their good fortune.

Already Foreigners

Two years after we made New Zealand our home, we returned back from a month back in Europe. Not for homesickness, but for the wedding of Jonathan, Laura's brother. The marriage was our reason to return, and without it we probably would have not gone back so soon, but it was an excellent opportunity to catch up with our family and friends. It also turned out to be an excellent way for us to look at our new life and compare it with our understanding of how our life might have been if we hadn't emigrated.

We arrived at Heathrow airport and immediately felt herded. None of the corridors seemed quite ready for use, the strip-lighting dangled worryingly by its own power cables, the signs seemed temporary and ambiguous, and I wondered what a new visitor to Britain must think of this dubious gateway to the country. The queue at the immigration hall was preceded by a queue to its doors. Once inside, the hall was a mass of shuffling families, the noise an intense hum. The smell was that of a thousand slightly tense, worn out travellers resigned to one more piece of processing before their lives could resume. Heaven forbid you might need the toilet!

It was an hour before the silent, overworked passport

inspector nodded us through. The feeling of being cattle didn't stop there, though. The roads, the shops, and the country in general had a feeling of crowdedness. I'd not noticed this when we lived in Britain but we both became aware of it quite quickly, not least because in the south east of England, it's at its most obvious. England, as the late, brilliant Vivian Stanshall poetically pointed out, is "changing yet changeless as canal water". This was apparent very quickly on our return to Britain. Nothing looked any different, it was, after all, only two years since we had left but, subtly, everything seemed slightly unfamiliar.

When confronted with this sense of unfamiliarity in a foreign land we expect and accept it, but when it's a place that used to be home, it feels a little dreamlike. You know the place and you can see past the superficial, but something remains odd and unsettling, as if you are an observer looking at a definition of familiar rather than the thing itself. This is one of the prices to be paid for migration, I've always been big-headed enough to pretend that the world is a small place and therefore it can all feel like home, but we are small animals, and our world view has evolved its own limits. We know what "Home" means. It's a feeling, not a location, and now home is a small and sparsely populated country in the South Pacific Ocean.

We both noticed that our own clocks had slowed down

and relative to us, the pace of life was faster than we were now used to. Not worse, just oddly different. It was wonderful to spend some real time with our families and our friends with whom we had kept in variable contact since we moved. Really good friends are always able to delete the gap since we last spent time together, taking the end of the last piece of togetherness and zipping it seamlessly to the next one, so that the intervening period vanished. We enjoyed ourselves hugely.

The wedding was in Ibiza, which gave us a real summer holiday in the middle of our winter but, strangely, we started to yearn for New Zealand rather earlier than we might have liked to admit and, by the time the month was up, we sorely missed our life here, animals, garden, friends and neighbours. We arrived back in Auckland to a similarly large queue in the immigration hall, just to prove that crowds are not a British monopoly, and after a long wait, we reached the passport inspector. He looked at our passports, stamped in our arrival dates, then looked at us, beamed and said,

"Welcome back!"

I wondered if he was the same lovely man who bade us welcome to New Zealand on our very first arrival.

Now, even that aspect of queuing has changed because New Zealand has introduced passports with RFID tags built into the booklet. All we do when we arrive back home is slot the passport into a computer, and a light that is strangely reminiscent of Hal in Kubrick's film 2001, stares at us for just a second too long, and we're in! I think maybe they should go the whole hog, and have a simulation of Hal's voice welcoming us back. "I'm sorry, Dave, I can't let you in..."

Canine Children

Bob the dog is a labradoodle. This is a cross (pun intended) he has to bear, that one of the loveliest, most people-centred breed of dog, with the intelligence of the poodle and the devoted affection of the handsome labrador, carries the silliest name of all breeds. OK, I know he's a mongrel really, and we wouldn't have it any other way, as I don't really approve of in-breeding, but by the time you read this there will no doubt be a society for labradoodles and a place for them at the posh and affected dog shows. Hopefully they will find a more appropriate name in keeping with nobility of these great dogs. My suggestion is treacle hound (as they are sweet and a wee bit thicker than you might expect).

Bob was born near Penrith in the north of England. His breeder, Carol, is a wonderful and diligent dog enthusiast and we were lucky to find her and her dogs. He's been a great companion and we certainly wouldn't have left the UK if we couldn't have taken him with us. As a couple, we had decided early on that we wanted to be childless, so he gets much of the attention and affection that we would probably otherwise have wasted on children. But the main difference is that he's more enthusiastic about retrieving a tennis ball than most teenagers. And his schooling is cheaper. And he sheds hairs everywhere. And he loves surfing and swimming (hmm, maybe he's not so different).

Bob grew up in the centre of Glasgow, with a pocket-sized shared garden and numerous walks in the park to occupy him. It must have been a shock for him to discover (after about a week of incarceration whilst he was flown over here) that he now has paddock after paddock of space to play in. He responded in just the way that you'd expect, by staying right by our side all the time. He loves to retrieve and will do so until exhausted and hyperthermic if we encourage him, but he's also cautious and lacking in sufficient self-confidence to run and play on his own. He was still a mere youth and needed a pal to play with, so we hadn't been in New Zealand more than six months before we started looking to find him a friend.

Brodie, from Whangarei, is a fleece coated example of the breed whereas Bob is a hairy coated 'doodle. Brodie doesn't shed his hairs but he does need constant grooming if his fur is to not to become completely matted and crusty. So he gets regular haircuts and shampoos. He's smaller than Bob, but his personality is massive. Unlike Bob, who is a little sensitive, Brodie has no notion of personal space, will cheerfully wander all over our feet, into knees, and cunningly occupy the position you were about to sit in on a couch milliseconds before you do. He has an excuse; when he was only twelve weeks old he was blinded in one eye in an awful incident when play with our friends' dog turned violent. Despite this, Brodie is the happiest, most enthusiastic dog you could meet, and obsessively devoted to Bob, whilst at the same time he 'cannae see green cheese' as the Glaswegian expression has it. (In case you're unaware of this brilliant expression, which so aptly suits Brodie (as he'd love even the greenest of cheeses) it simply means that if you see someone with something good, you have to have it too). Bob and Brodie play really well together, Bob being significantly larger than his young sibling, balanced against Brodie's almost infuriating tenacity and a dazzling turn of speed. At first we thought we could get on with the gardening, running of the farm and all the usual chores of living in the countryside without being shadowed by Bob needing our attention. But no, now both Bob and Brodie shadow us.

Dog owning in New Zealand is different from Scotland. In Scotland there is a "right to roam" that makes damage to property illegal, but there's no law of trespass. All beaches are public property and dogs are generally permitted everywhere as long as they are under control. In New Zealand, beaches and the countryside are often private and not the rambler's paradise that I had imagined they might be before we arrived. There are some brilliant places to walk, but many of them exclude the presence of dogs, often for sound ecological reasons. Before the presence of people here, the only mammals were bats and almost all the wildlife was avian. So any areas that fall under the aegis of the Department of Conservation are unlikely to welcome dogs to ensure that the birds, especially the flightless kiwi, are protected. The consequence of this for us dog owners is that we have to be very selective when it comes to days out in the countryside away from home. Although the list is dwindling, there are some superb beaches nearby that are dog friendly as long as the basic rules of consideration are followed (keeping the animals and their excrement under control), but many forest walks and wild areas are for people and their invisible parasites only. We had heard some stories before we arrived of people returning to the UK because New Zealand was not dog friendly. Although we haven't found that, we have experienced a more pragmatic attitude towards the canine members of society than we noticed in Britain. There are far more working dogs here, if you take into consideration farm dogs and pig dogs (what they hunt, not what they look like).

The ideal place for walking and playing with dogs is the beach, and we have two very enthusiastic companions for any day out that includes sun, surf, sand and sticks. Bob may be sensitive on land, but show him some massive breakers and he's in heaven, swimming out after far-flung sticks and timing his return with an expert surfer's precision, cresting huge waves with a big grin on his face. Brodie is far more cautious of the surf and happier to retrieve land-based sticks, but he's only a pup. These two canine children of ours add immeasurably to our quality of life, and without them our paradise would seem a little emptier. They were certainly one of the main reasons for our homesickness when we went back to Europe for a month! Fortunately for our future holidays, we now seem to have acquired regular offers for house sitting, pets, livestock and all, so we don't have to feel trapped in the idyll with which we have surrounded ourselves.

A year after Brodie joined the family, Laura saw a space in our lives, not occupied by Bob and Brodie, which was the shape of a female dog. She knew the dog existed, and she knew it was a Labradoodle, that it was chocolate brown, and that it lived nearby. She looked at "Trade-me" (the NZ equivalent of Ebay) adverts, SPCA notices and small ads at the supermarket. Eventually she found a dog looking for a home as the owners were moving to Auckland and couldn't have the dog, a year old bitch, in their new apartment. She contacted the owners, who told her that she'd just missed her chance. A housebound elderly lady was looking for a companion dog, and theirs fitted the bill perfectly. We were a little disappointed. Laura was so sure she had a feeling that this was to be our third dog, and her intuition, much to the annoyance of my scientific views, was rarely wrong. We were also a little surprised, knowing as we do, that Labradoodle pups are bouncy, energetic and enthusiastic, and need lots of attention and play.

Three days later the former owners of the dog emailed Laura to say that, as we suspected, the elderly lady really needed something more calm and gentle. And so we dashed off to Helensville to meet our new pup. When we arrived we were bowled over. Almost literally. Talulah, (or Lulah for short) even as a pup, was considerably taller than the two boys. We suspected that she might not be exactly just poodle and labrador, but maybe a bit of hound, too. Irish wolfhound, perhaps. To start with, she's fast, twice as fast even than Brodie, and she is thin, supermodel thin. Even though we feed her twice as much as Bob and Brodie, she never puts on weight.

She came home with us that evening, sitting in the back seat of the car, looking forlorn, and whining softly. She was going to miss her old home, the other two dogs she ran with, and the seven year old boy who loved her. We felt very sorry for her, but knew that she'd be fine quite soon. That night she wouldn't settle, she paced, whined and cried and we couldn't sleep. Eventually, we put her on our bed and, much to our delight, she settled in between us, grinned and fell asleep in a minute. Sneaky bitch.

The next day, we introduced her to the art of retrieving,

something that all dogs with a trace of labrador know instinctively. She couldn't believe her luck, and we couldn't believe her speed. It was immediately apparent that we'd needed to distract her with her own ball while we threw for the other two dogs. Otherwise, she'd race and catch her ball, and immediately drop it, chase after the other balls and sometimes even stuff two or even three tennis balls into her mouth at the same time.

She's been with us a year now, and has become very much part of the family. She's still nutty, and enough of a puppy that she loves to carry around a favourite toy wherever she goes until she decides to rip it to shreds, at which point we dispose of it, and find another unwanted stuffed toy at the SPCA, which she nurses like a mother for a few weeks, and then the cycle repeats itself. She loves to be hugged, preferably to the point where she's sitting on your knee, which is a neat trick with a dog that weighs thirty kilos and stands as tall as Naomi Campbell. And she loves to swim. She swims like a mad thing and knows no fear. In fact, when we first introduced her to the stream that runs through the farm, we feared for her safety; we threw a stick in the time honoured way and, before Bob had a chance to work his way into the water (which is quite shallow), Lulah had leapt into the water, all four legs splayed, a great grin on her face and a massive belly-flop. The stick was not important, it was dropped as soon as it was found, but the sprint up the river bank and the launch, that was the fun of it, and her exuberance was astonishing.

The three dogs make a good pack. Bob is the calm patriarch these days, getting his own way because he knows how to, with selective hearing when admonished. Brodie is a little charmer, very affectionate and cute, but with a killing streak that means that the chickens have to stay in their run, while Lulah is the mad youth, up first every morning, wagging her tail against the bedroom wall like a metronome. They make a good team.

A Moving House Story

In an earlier chapter, I've written about the day trip to Dargaville with our friends who were looking to relocate a house onto their block of land by the sea. The venerable villa they found was, in the end, deemed suitable for the purpose and a house moving company, Haines, were contracted to do the deed. You rarely see houses being shifted along the roads in this part of New Zealand. There's a good reason for this; they take up most of both carriageways, consequently most of the moving is done in the depth of night.

Because the final site for the house was down a steep hill, near a drop-off to the sea, the track to the site had needed careful preparation and a deep cut through the clay soil of the section had been prepared. This moving operation calls for the best of weather conditions if the newly exposed clay is not to be churned up into the most glutinous, gumbootsucking substance that nature can create. So it was with some relief that the night dusked clear and cool. A posse of at least a dozen of us were on alert to watch the house as it arrived in Kerikeri. The men from Haines had told us that the fastest the house could be moved was eighty kilometres an hour – I was astonished that the trucks could even move this rapidly.

And so, at three o'clock on a chilly morning in April, with thermos or bottle to hand, we waited with anticipation until the most extraordinary procession I have ever seen gradually appeared out of the night. The first sign of the convoy was the flashing orange lights of the advance truck, there to warn any passing motorist that a mobile, multi-tonne, contemporary art installation was heading their way. Then, lumbering towards us as we stood and applauded on a roundabout, came the house, now divided into three sections and looking like architectural dinosaur snails.

As if to emphasise the notion that the beasts were alive, as the first truck reached a road sign with which it must surely collide, so massive was its girth, it reared up on one side, lifting the house clear over the sign before it hydraulically sighed, and returned to its usual height. Passing us, lit by the streetlights and orange strobes, it then ambled off into the night and the process repeated itself with the next section. Soon they were gone and, with a dreamlike memory of their passing, we grinned, toasted the house and each other from hip-flasks and cheerfully went home.

The next day it poured with rain. Nothing could be done to move the sections of house that now stood forlornly at the top of the hill. Conditions had become too dangerous to guarantee the safe passage of the house to its intended resting place. The men from Haines seemed unperturbed, they must have seen this many times before, and so we waited, hoping the rain was not seeping through the tarpaulins that covered the exposed rooms of the house. Three days later the weather came right, and off the house pieces went at a breakneck two kilometres an hour. Even at this low speed, the progress was amazing if not a little unnerving. At one hairpin bend, the divided pieces were winched round, towed by a massive Tonka-like bulldozer that sat on its “heels” to take the strain. The usually unflappable house movers looked a little unnerved at one point when part of the house made a bid for freedom and, for a brief moment, appeared to be running away to sea, but it was tamed, brought back into line and redirected along the gloopy track. Candidly, one of the usually taciturn Maori drivers turned to me and said,

“I think that’s the closest we’ve ever come to losing a house!”

Finally, a day later, the component pieces of the house we’d once visited as a gloomy retirement home in Dargaville came together on a sun-baked promontory on the other side of the island and, by some New Zealand cunning and ingenuity, the house was stitched back again almost seamlessly. It looked as if it had been simply carried by some giant’s hand from its urban origins to its new location by the sea.

So impressed were we by this display of Kiwi bravura that, a few months later, we decided to add a small cottage to the buildings on our little farm and call it The Acorn. Now, not only has The Acorn given us wonderful accommodation for Laura's family, in between visits we rent it out as a holiday house to visitors to the area. We're gradually planting the garden around it (it just sits in a paddock) so that, in time it will look like its been here forever!

The Acorn

Laura's parents were keen to come over on a regular basis and share our lovely life, like Aberdonian swallows, flying over here for a few months of summer. We thought we could organise the building of a little bach but whichever way we looked, the prices were either really steep, or the construction was that of a glorified tin shed. Compared to the cost of relocating an older house, the new-builds didn't make any sense. Finding a tiny cottage should have been easy, but in the end had more to do with luck than persistence. Eventually we found a really cute, 1950s house built almost entirely of Rimu, a locally felled and very attractive timber. The cottage was full of character, still retaining all the '50s features such as the hand built kitchen and solid wood floors. In keeping with New Zealand tradition, there was no insulation, so we've now added that.

With none of the drama of our friends' house, "The Acorn" was transported sixty kilometres up the road, placed gently on the new foundation posts and then decorated in about seventeen seconds. (When Laura gets a bee in her bonnet about decorating, it's tiring even to watch!). We had really wanted to repeat the midnight vigil to see the house arrive, but it was so small, requiring only one truck and no chainsaw, that we never even noticed until it was at the farm gate two hours early! It was a delight to see the Haines men again, and this time so relaxed with a simple, stress free move.

Laura had been agonizing over the precise positioning of the cottage. Council regulations determine how close it can come to the neighbour's boundary, and at the last minute she was worried that it was too close. So, the night before the cottage arrived, she surreptitiously moved the marker pegs that told the guys where to put the house. Then she panicked in case they looked at what she'd done and refused to put the house there. They didn't care.

"You can put the house wherever you like as long as it's reasonably flat." they said.

The garden around The Acorn is now well-established, and the house looks less plonked onto a paddock than before. A post and rail fence surrounds it, and a grassy road leads to it so that the occupants don't have to open farm gates or be inconvenienced by friendly livestock. The cottage has become a real asset to the home. Laura's mum and dad come and stay from time to time, especially her mother who has visited so many times that the airline knows her by her first name, and she always brings good weather. This is the purpose for which the house was moved here in the first place, as a second home for them. Beyond that, we rent the cottage to holidaymakers over the summer; usually a few days at a time, and having got used to the fact that, although we are not officially in the Bay of Islands and the views are entirely pastoral, they delight in the tranquillity of the place and the very slow pace of life. We are in the sub-tropical south Pacific, after all!

Lately, we have discovered there is a huge demand from budget travellers for accommodation in exchange for hard work. An online organisation called Helpx provides an international database that lists home owners and gives them a chance to describe their place and the work they need doing. In turn, this allows potential guests to contact the hosts and arrange the accommodation. It's a great system, and through it, we've been delighted to host many young people who stay in the cottage, work a few hours per day, and see the far north of New Zealand without breaking the bank. Armed with a list of all the jobs we would otherwise never quite get around to, we delegate the removal of pasture weeds (thistles, gorse, nettles - who put those there?) to these visitors. Painting the house? No problem. Chopping wood for the winter? The job is yours, and my back thanks you. There is another organisation, 'Wwoofers' by name, that does a similar job, but is primarily aimed at willing workers on organic farms (oh, look, there goes an acronym), and since we're not entirely organic, we didn't want to mislead anyone.

We used to look at other properties (well, some of them, not that one over there with the rusting old cars) and wonder how much work went into keeping the place looking so pristine. Now we gaze at the newly extended chicken run, or the bright paint on the verandah, and chuckle knowingly whilst we think up ever more esoteric jobs to be done. Actually, that last bit is rubbish. Nobody we know chuckles knowingly, and the jobs remain resolutely down to earth and just keep on coming. After all, you can never have too much firewood, and the gum trees that were planted around the perimeter of the farm have a habit of suddenly dying and losing branches.

Meanwhile The Acorn, despite being used most of the year round, carries a sense of holiday-house charm, and no one who has stayed there has wanted to leave early. Indeed, some of the holidaymakers just seem to buy food and drink and do little more than sit on the deck and relax. And, in a sense (as a great film critic was wont to say) why not?

Artichokes, thousands of 'em

We arrived in New Zealand as green-fingered as most urbanites. That is to say, not in the slightest. We were happy to take the risk that, out of this deep well of ignorance, we might be able to draw sufficient instinctive understanding of what it takes to grow food. It was both daunting and inspiring when we found, under the weeds, a really well tended, and established organic and biodynamic garden and smallholding. Of course, we did see all that before we bought the farm, but it always looks easier when the maintenance is day to day and organised. Especially if someone else has done all the work. Now it was our problem and catching up with the weeds was vital.

Well, it turned out that, despite her inexperience and aided and abetted by her enthusiasm, Laura is a natural at the gardening thing. Our veggie garden rapidly went from a ten square metre plot of random chaos and evil to a productive and pretty area of raised beds, mulch and green veggie heaven. Beyond the vegetable patch, in one of the paddocks close to the house was a huge crop of artichokes. The previous owners, who were lovely people and enthusiastic gardeners, had noticed that the dark rich volcanic loam of the area is a great place for thistles to grow, and no matter how much you cut them down, they just come straight back up again like some kind of Ray Harryhausen monster. The sensible thing to do is to grow thistles. So that's what they did; huge, edible Mediterranean thistles otherwise known as globe artichokes. There was about half an acre of them and, come the fruiting season, which is most of spring and summer, they would pick hundreds of these prickly delicacies and sell them at the local farmers market.

We saw this as a challenge. Surely we could do at least as well with this crop. After all, it is just a glorified weed. To this end, we insisted that the property sale included the old Massey Ferguson tractor and slasher, without which tending to these beauties would be a real chore. Since we arrived in early October, the spring had sprung, and with it the artichokes. We duly picked them, and realised that this horticulture thing wasn't simply a matter of growing veggies and taking them to market; we would have to make some contacts to help us. And so we met Claire. She is the queen of down to earth, a lovely person, both pragmatic and emotional simultaneously. She seems to know everyone in Northland, and has a stall at the weekly market in Kerikeri (described in the next chapter) where she sells beautiful herbs for cooking and growing. Her enthusiasm for plants, and her encouragement for our novice efforts helped immensely, and our confidence did the same thing as the artichokes. Week after week as summer arrived, our baskets of artichokes sold, those that were surplus always found their way to some friends for dinner. We felt we were really farming! And we'd only been here a few months.

At the end of the season, with the plants wilting and putting on a final show of immense purple thistle flowers (which, it transpired, are almost as popular in the market as the edible head), we fired up Billy the tractor and slashed them all down to the ground. Whilst I got the hang of the tractor, being quite inexperienced compared with Laura, she took photo after photo of the event. We looked so much as if we knew what we were doing it was brilliant! And then we had a field full of dead plants. What had we done? I know the previous owners said they need to be slashed back (then they decompose and feed the soil), but what if they were taking the piss? So we waited.

The following spring, and with no uncertainty, up they came, hardy, silver-green and bursting with life. And while we'd never planned to be artichoke growers, and despite the fact that Laura doesn't even like the taste of them, nothing could have made us prouder nor more part of the community here than the fact that we produce something that other people appreciate and will pay for.

The Sunday Market

Farmers' Markets have become a very popular phenomenon. It's hardly surprising; well cultivated produce, made by people who care as much about the quality of what they make as the amount they make for it, will always attract buyers. In Kerikeri, there are plenty of people who can afford the time and the (sometimes) increased prices of the produce, so all year round the market, every Sunday morning, is a busy place. And what a wonderful place it is. In true street market style, it is so much more than the sum of its parts. And the parts (or stalls, as I like to call them) are really wonderful in themselves. There's music from a variety of live bands (one at a time is how I prefer them) of such quality that they are a feature in their own right. There's such a plethora of producers that we consumers are spoilt for choice. There's food for breakfast; crepes, German-recipe sausages on the barbecue, mussel fritters, cooked sandwiches and even cakes and macadamia nut cookies. There's a coffee stand with beautifully crafted flat whites (that's New Zealand speak for a kind of café latte, but with less milk, and a stretched froth (In case you couldn't tell, New Zealanders take their coffee very seriously)) made from locally roasted coffee. Then there's the produce, the freshest of fruit from the exotic custard apple, pineapple and tamarillo to the more expected apple, avocado and citrus fruit; veggies in abundance and all in their season, organic, spray free or simply well cared-for.

There are locally made cheeses from an expert family business originally from the Netherlands, so that award-winning gouda and edam are much in evidence, salamis from an Austrian master, chilli sauces including the fearsome Bhut Jolokia, and artisan bread that sells out in about ten minutes. There's a stall selling fresh and smoked fish and even their own bottled and preserved tuna, a couple of local winemakers with a glug of breakfast tastings and even a local sherry and port maker, whose wares I'm particularly fond of. Since when was a drop of very cold dry sherry out of date? Ask a Spaniard! There are jam and pickle makers whose bejewelled jars catch the light and a fresh juice seller, who freezes his wares in the summer, to the delight of the children wandering round the stalls.

I'm very fond of Claire's stall selling fresh herbs for planting out (or using straight away). She loves her plants and those we buy from her always thrive in our garden. In addition to the herbs, she also has a thriving business selling Vetiver plants. These grasses put down extraordinarily long roots that can stabilise the soil and prevent erosion. In a coastal region, especially where housing development has denuded the native bush in order to actually see the sea, erosion is a real problem and, when it pours, landslips are not uncommon. Vetiver can rapidly lock in some of this weakened clay soil and allow other plants to take root. It's a great idea and one gaining in popularity as more people set their sights on a chance to live by the sea. Claire, as I've already mentioned, also sells our artichokes. A big basket, delivered first thing on a Sunday morning, will be down to the last few sad looking globes within a couple of hours. The demand for them is quite surprising considering how easy we find them to grow.

The market is such a great place to meet friends. Indeed, on some Sunday mornings, that seems to be all we have time for. We never seem to quite get around the stalls as, with every second step, we bump into friends and acquaintances, catch up on news and gossip, discuss the week to come, and wonder where our Sunday went! In the sunshine, on a busy day, it's the hub of Kerikeri's community while on a rainy day, only the diehard locals will be there, sheltering under tarpaulins and keeping their heads down. But at all times, it's a reminder of what so many people yearn for in their daily lives; the sense of belonging and being part of something.

Farming!

Twenty-two acres is a lot of garden, and when we first arrived we soon realised that our combination of ignorance and enthusiasm was potentially a source of harm to our newly acquired land, and a source of great mirth for our neighbours. We hadn't banked on the expertise of Dwayne, a local farmer who came to our rescue. Dwayne certainly breaks the stereotypical farmer's mould. Sure, initially, he seems the part, with battered truck, faded clothes and a truly laconic manner, but then you start to notice subtle hints that there's more to him than you first think. He's optimistic – I'm not saying that optimism is rare in farmers, but in Dwayne's case it means that he's happy regardless of the weather, he rarely moans about potential bad news and genuinely seems happy with his life. He also has a softness for his working dogs that I've never encountered in a farmer before. The way he treats them, you'd swear that they are his pets!

So Dwayne took on the task of making the land work for us. It may be a big garden, but it's a very small farm, and we were delighted when we found ourselves the proud custodians of twenty two young bulls (you may remember I mentioned them when we first moved in). They seemed a little aloof, but they were probably just getting used to us.

Clearly, we weren't about to give them all names, as we knew that we'd have to say goodbye to them before too long. Gradually these black angus calves grew up on the good grass paddocks, looking strong and healthy.

Dwayne and his wife Tanya had a baby girl and decided to buy a farm about an hour's drive away, and so it became our task, every few days, to move the bullocks from one paddock to the next. We noticed that they were growing horns and other appendages, and the word calf was no longer appropriate. Dwayne and his dad appeared at the farm gate one day planning to de-horn his herd. They wanted to know if we'd like to watch or even help. Sadly (yeah, right) we had to decline, as we were on our way out for the day and, on our return, we decided that avoiding this particular aspect of farm life was definitely a good thing. The stockyard was splattered with blood and a pile of horns was a constant lure to the dogs who wasted no time in finding ways into the yard until we bagged the horns and found a local biodynamic farmer who wanted them for whatever arcane purposes biodynamic farmers have for cow horns. Of all the animals, only one beast, that Dwayne was looking after for a neighbour, remained intact, a fine Hereford bullock of slightly smaller stature than his Angus pals. He was far friendlier than the others, happy to come to us and lick our hands and Laura had named him Boris.

The de-horning must have caused some noise, broadcast locally (or cattle have a version of Facebook that we're not privy to) because within a day of the operation, two yearling heifers appeared on the scene, having pushed through several fences to join us, or more specifically to join a herd of noisy, irritable, slightly sore but nevertheless very randy young bulls. And I suspect that the commotion that followed for the next few days was just as dramatic.

There are a few established ways to find the owners of livestock if it arrives on your land. We checked to see if the beasts had any identification, but these two were travelling incognito. Then we visited all the local farmers and drew blanks. We phoned the agriculture information service run by the local council to see if anyone had reported the animals missing, but nobody had. Our neighbours suggested that, if no one claimed the cows, it was a bovine bonus for us. Three weeks after they appeared, a farmer from about two kilometres away called to say that she had heard that we might have her cows. Sure enough, they had, in an act of hormonal exuberance, crossed three farms in order to be with the noisiest bulls in Northland. She seemed entirely nonplussed by this feat, but I suspect that nonplussed was her middle name, as she seemed even less talkative than Dwayne. She arrived with a small truck, herded her beasts into it, and drove off without even a murmur of apology or thanks. Nowadays, we'd know better and attach an invoice for the grazing and insemination service to the backside of one of the cows.

Once the heifers had left, we anticipated that the bulls would return to their usual discreet lowing, but no, the forbidden fruit had been tasted. Now they would make the most terrible and primitive of noises almost every night, they would lean on rail fences and break them and, at two years old and about eight hundred kilos, they became a little difficult to manage. We spoke to friends, neighbours and patients, and everybody had a similar opinion, nobody in their right mind would keep twenty two sex-mad bulls on a small "lifestyle block"! We spoke to Dwayne who agreed;

"I've never tried keeping as many bulls as this before! I reckon that it's about time I took them away," he said, rather wistfully.

So it was decided that the bulls should go, and now that he was busy with his own farm and new family, we should find another farmer to run the grazing, someone more locally based, so that we didn't have to take quite so much responsibility for the farming we were pretending to manage.

All of a sudden we were down to two beasts, Boris, who was now Laura's constant pastoral companion together with an anonymous angus bull, who was destined for the homekill expert and thence the freezer. Dwayne organised the deed, warning us that it would be first thing in the morning. But he didn't specify which morning. A few days later we woke to the sound of a gunshot. It was about half past six, misty and damp. The bull had been killed and, while in theory I would rather like to have seen it happen, as I feel strongly that we should not ignore the process whereby we get our meat, I didn't want to leave the warmth of our bed to brave the grey autumn morning to see butchery done. I've never said I'm not a hypocrite. The butcher was an expert and swift. By half past seven he was gone, but then we discovered that so had Boris. We still had the angus bull (was that a look of relief on his face?) but Laura's lovely pal (she was hoping to ask the owner if we could buy him as a pet) was gone and bound for the freezer.

This was a tragic day in our brief, naive farming life. Laura was beside herself. We had told ourselves right from the start that we would not become emotionally attached to any stock that might be destined for our plate, but that had been taken out of our hands by a piece of ghastly miscommunication. Floods of tears ensued. There was only one thing for it. Laura was clear on this. We would have to find a kitten, and quickly. I wasn't entirely surprised to discover that the feline research had already been done. There was a farm near Taipa with long-haired grey tabbies available, and a short drive confirmed that they were indeed, registering close to ten on the relative cuteness scale. And so the kitten came home with us. Not only did she turn out to be the most friendly, placid and crazy bundle of purr, but she also turned out to be male and impossible to name. Temporarily, and for his relaxed demeanour, we named him Freaky, but our vet won't have a bar of it. That's OK, he responds to anything.

There is a very sad footnote to this story. Cats are not gregarious by nature, and very territorial in their behaviour. Whilst Freaky was a welcome addition to our household, the other cats (all four of them) decided that our favouritism to him in the house would be reflected by excluding him from the garden, and to establish his territory he would have to venture further afield. One dismal morning, we knew something was wrong when he didn't greet us in his habitual way in the kitchen. We couldn't find him anywhere, but our neighbour, returning from her Saturday walk, had seen him on the main road verge, lifeless. We buried him in tears and soil, and momentarily wondered if the joy that affectionate animals brings with them is worth the pain of their loss. The other cats responded (even before we knew he was gone) with a total change of behaviour. They became relaxed, friendly and spirited. And we realised that there had been a feline tension that Freaky had brought with him, and we had never noticed. He was just one cat too many.

Trees and Heifers

Grant is the new farmer who looks after and rents the pasture. He's very tall, wears (as is the uniform around here) the shortest of shorts, and is the very definition of the word "wiry". He has a great but arid sense of humour and also has the traditional farmer's knack for seeing every aspect of nature as a personal challenge. If the sun's shining, then it's getting a bit dry. If it's raining, then that's not going to help get the tractor about, now is it? He knows what he's like, and, if you ever suggest to him that he's being a little pessimistic, then he'll smile wryly and admit his foible.

Grant is an enthusiastic fence builder and his first task when he became farmer-in-residence (can you tell that I used to run an art gallery?) was to rebuild and repair some of our more worn out fences. This in turn led us to look at the vast number of trees on our property. He and I wandered gently around the boundary, eyeing up the trees. I was immensely proud of them, he just seemed very worried:

"I reckon the best thing would be to take out all of the biggest ones first; they'll be worth something as timber, and then we can cut all the others down for firewood, " he suggested.

All the paddocks were bounded and divided by shelterbelt, as it is known, consisting of gum trees, macrocarpa (known elsewhere as Monterey Cypress) and poplars. This shelterbelt is a relic from the time when all the farmland was orchard, and required much protection from the prevailing winds, and now he wanted to remove as many of the old ones as possible. Despite my love of trees, by the time we'd beaten the bounds, he had me quite convinced, albeit with a capsized and sinking heart, that if we did nothing to them then they would, at the very least, walk up to the house and steal our cats. In reality he was concerned that, if any of them fell, they would damage his newly repaired fences and short the electric circuit.

Fortunately, Laura loves the trees as much as I do and she wondered why it wouldn't be easier just to repair the fences if we did have any unexpected disarbours (I just made that word up). Grant backtracked and explained that it was only his opinion and, if we wanted to keep the trees, that would be just fine. So the trees are staying. But even then, right at the outset of our relationship with Grant, there was was this little moment, this slight feeling that maybe he was not entirely on our side.

Once all the fences were fixed, it was time to put some more stock on the land. Laura accompanied Grant to the weekly stock auction in Kaikohe to find some "empty" heifers. Farming terminology is the argot in this part of the world, so I knew that heifers are young female cows that have never had a calf. Empty ones, as you might expect, aren't pregnant. The cows arrived in small batches, first came a truck with five lovely little Aberdeen Angus cows, black, friendly and inquisitive. A week later we had six more heifers, this time Hereford/Friesian crosses, with the furrowed brow of the Hereford. Finally, a few weeks later some very pretty Charolais made the number up to nineteen. They settled in remarkably well for a day, and then three of the Charolais disappeared. Grant was very upset. The cost of these beasts is not small, and the fences were obviously in excellent shape. Where could the cows have gone? We phoned around the neighbours, walked and then drove further afield to see if we could espy them and, by the time a week had passed, Grant was pretty convinced that they had been rustled. But then, after a helpful call from a neighbour, we found them about two kilometres away, happily munching someone else's grass! We dashed over, with Grant shouting into a cellphone, arranging a stock truck as we went. When we arrived within sight of the cows, they moved discreetly away, and, after about twenty minutes of gentle organised stalking, followed by another twenty minutes of frantic, sweaty chasing, it became obvious that they had the measure of us and were in no mood to be herded.

Disillusioned, we returned to the house to plan a

second attempt, only to find that the heifers had, in their enthusiasm for trickery, returned back to the paddock from which they escaped. We reunited them with their herd (they now seemed curiously docile) and they stayed content with their boundaries thereafter. Oddly, we could find no break in the fence or current that would have allowed their little peregrination.

A few weeks later, it became clear that three of the heifers weren't as empty as they were supposed to be and no, it wasn't the wandering Charolais, but three of the Hereford crosses. Grant was characteristically disgruntled, as he didn't know if the sire of these calves to be was a large breed of bull, which might cause some birthing problems for the little cows. Everyone else thought it was brilliant news. Three free calves! Laura and I were delighted, but a bit worried by Grant's concern. We'd be the ones who would have to take some action if the delivery became complicated. We waited and tried to second-guess the due date. And then, one misty morning, Caspar arrived, grey as a ghost. When we first saw her, she was tottering and leggy, still damp, but confident and feeding, and all was well. Our first home birth! We took hundreds of photos, as proud as anything that everything had gone well. Maybe we shouldn't have named her as she would be going away to slaughter eventually, but she wouldn't be our homekill, so we wouldn't have quite the same attachment as we had to Boris. The other two heifers also calved without fuss and away from our prying eyes. Despite the presence of the calves being outside Grant's plan for the herd he did, in fact, seem quite happy with them. He'd just never admit it.

Keeping Cattle

Sooner or later, it made sense to us that, if there were going to be some cattle raised on our land, they should be raised by us and not for other people. We'd had rented the paddocks to a couple of graziers and had watched them carry out the various tasks that were needed, the maintenance of fences, the cleaning of weeds from the pasture, and the whole process of ensuring that the cattle were well fed, well tended, healthy and generally happy. So now it was our turn.

Grant had removed his beasts in late August, traditionally the time to sell cattle, and we had decided to put some steers onto the property in November, allowing for an excellent spring pasture growth. We called upon the help of some friends we had made over the time we had been here and decided on a two-pronged investment. We would raise a couple of Highland cows as pets, for the beauty and nature of them, and some steers for fattening and thence to slaughter. The Highland cattle were being raised by a couple of expert farmers on the other side of Kerikeri who were close to dismantling their herd as part of their plans for retirement. We chose a very young black steer and his yearling red-haired sister. And so Aoife and Ruairidh became the first of the Darroch fold! With

Ruairidh being only marginally bigger than the dogs, they made a very cute pair, and we knew we'd chosen well. Another farming couple, who we knew well from a few kilometres up the road, had a small dairy farm and wanted to sell off their weaner steers. At about three months old, these were also tiny and very friendly, having been bottle reared so that their mothers could be milked. We chose nine of them, wanting to ensure that we had more than enough grazing for them all (as a rule of thumb, one animal per acre is pretty much sustainable all year long, and we have about eighteen acres of useful pasture). And so, one morning, the cattle truck arrived with our miniature herd! As they were about the same age, we put them in with the Highland cattle, where they thrived, growing almost as we watched.

Gradually, it became apparent that the steers, all dairy cross-breeds, were developing in a very different way from the Highlands. The steers are quite dainty, almost feminine and affectionate. One of them loved having the buds, where his horns would have been, scratched, and was very amenable to human contact. In fact, and despite advice to the contrary, Laura had all of them named within minutes of them arriving, and clearly would need to be absent from the farm when the truck arrived to take them away to be sold. On the other hand, the Highland cattle were feisty and nervous. They loved the odd bucket of "Moosli", a molasses-based cattle feed, and were a formidable sight now that their horns had passed the thirty centimetre mark. They bellowed, pranced, and rushed at us, only to stop with a skid less than a metre away. Like unruly children, if they weren't shown some discipline, they would take their exuberance too far, and then it would end in tears. Also, they bullied the steers. Every time we moved them from one paddock to the next, Aoife would stand at the gate in an attempt to bar their progress, whilst Ruairidh took up the rear and threatened to impale any laggards. The final straw came when we realised that one of the steers had been marked as if it were a flashy car that has inspired envy in someone with a set of keys, so in the end we had to separate them.

About six months later, another addition to the fold arrived. Candy was a seventeen year old Highland cow with the biggest horns ever seen. She also had the widest belly, and our friends the experts, knowing she was pregnant (for the sixteenth time) couldn't bring themselves to send her to the works, having reared her from a calf. Knowing how soft hearted we are, they asked if we would look after her. Of course we were honoured and delighted. She was magnificent, slightly timid, and an incorrigible mother. Three months later Lachlan McYoda, aka Lachie, was born (he looked like the small furry monk from the Star Wars films). He was soon taller than the dogs, and alternated between the timidity of his mum and the curiosity of the young. Eventually, we introduced him to his niece and nephew (Candy is Aoife's grandmother!) but only after we had established a little more discipline in the young scallywags. The decision to undergraze the property was made out of caution as we were new to the whole business of actual farming, but, as the year wore on, it became clear that it had been an accidentally sound decision. From October until March the following year, barely a drop of rain fell. From the point of view of recreation, it was the best summer ever with warm nights and long hot days, but from a farming perspective it was the worst drought Northland had seen in many years. All around us the farmland turned brown, reminiscent of the landscape I had become accustomed to in Australia, and more and more farmers had to sell their herds in fear for their welfare. Because we had legal access to a stream that runs through our property, so our water troughs never run dry, and because of the small number of animals we had on the pasture, our farm momentarily looked like an island of green in the midst of all that brown. We were very relieved that there was no risk to the growing calves and they flourished in the summer sun. The following winter showed little signs of making up for the summer drought, and the water table was now lower than it should be for spring. But the grass was growing at high speed and all around, the pasture became once again the lush, green fields of New Zealand.

However, the Highland cattle were fast becoming an issue. We had treated them with so much kindness and no sense of discipline, that their inner teenager was starting to rebel. On the day that we had arranged to have Lachie's maleness curtailed, we had all four of the Highlanders in the stockyard (they had become inseparable once they all were in the same paddock together). I was in there too, marshalling Lachie into the crush so that the vet could get close to him, and keeping the other three back. Just as I managed to persuade Lachie into the narrow corridor that leads to the crush, I saw Ruairidh out of the corner of my eye, turning rapidly towards me with his head down. He has the forward pointing horns of a fighting bull and, without thinking, I was up, and over the yard fence - not propelled by him, thankfully, but vaulting for my life as one of the points tore my shirt. I really didn't think there was malice in Ruairidh's behaviour, he was sure there must be food where I was; I had the feed bucket with me. However, I was now nervous of him, whereas before I has been merely cautious. So, a few days later, when we had a call from our neighbour, Jean, telling us that Aoife and Ruairidh were in her paddock, my heart sank a little. Firstly because I knew that getting them back to our fields would be tricky (the gate was at the other end of Jean's farm), but secondly because I knew that something was going to have to be done so that I could feel comfortable with them again. We wandered down to the far paddock and saw that a tree had fallen across the fence allowing the Highlanders egress. Beyond the fence was an old, tumbledown stone wall, the true boundary of our land, and beyond that, mooing contentedly and munching the low hanging branches of a poplar, were the cattle. Standing at the paddock gate about five hundred metres away, I shook the feed bucket in a halfhearted attempt to distract them. We were both surprised when they looked up, saw us and, without hesitation, they were over the wall, over the broken fence and charging towards us like beserker vikings. We dumped the Moosli, got through the gate and turned to see them skidding to a halt, nose already deep in feed. That night, I contacted the Highland Cattle Association to speak to someone with much more experience than we had, to get some advice on how to deal with two very enthusiastic cattle. One option was to remove their long and pointy horns, but that was quickly rejected as it can cause a great deal of pain, significant blood loss, and psychological trauma. All the other suggestions were along the lines of much stricter discipline and halter training for the cattle and, to be honest, neither of us felt we wanted to go down that path. So we asked ourselves what we were doing with them, if all the joy of looking after them was fast draining away. Around that time, we met Steve. He had recently moved into a property with a few acres of land and had come to lay a new drain to the septic tank. He is a horse breeder but also had a Jersey house cow. We told him about our cattle and the problems they were bringing us. We suggested he might like to take them off our hands, what with all that land he just bought. I was joking. But he didn't think I was, in fact he was delighted! The next day, he brought his wife over to see the cattle. She too was delighted. She'd always wanted Highland cattle, and this was too good an opportunity to miss. And so their good fortune became ours too, and we could rest easy, knowing that they were moving to a lovely new home.

And now we know why all the markets insist that cattle should be dehorned before going to be sold. The cattle truck arrived, and the driver helped us to guide the four of them into the correct race to go up the ramp into the truck. Every post became an obstacle for the horns and despite my nervousness, and with infinite gratitude to the stockman for his help, it took nearly an hour and some serious manhandling of the cattle before they were finally on their way.

Hypnotizing Chickens

Let nobody tell you that chickens are boring. And while we're at it, let no one tell you that they are dimwitted. Chickens (and all other expressions of nature, for that matter) are exactly as intelligent as they need to be. They couldn't survive any other way. But chickens are fun!

The garden was becoming well organised, and Laura was, at last, starting to feel that she was on top of the veggie production requirements and the Herculean weeding task. For most people, that would mean an opportunity to do a little less work and to take things a bit easier, but for Laura, this turn of events signalled a chance to expand another part of the garden, and she turned her attention to the long overgrown chicken run. We had inherited a very comfortable (in fowl terms) hen house with laying stalls, roosting perches and a weatherproof tin roof. This was situated in a well-proportioned run, surrounded, for the most part, by netting and chicken wire. All it would need was a wee trim of the bigger bushes, some tidying up and a clean out of the hen house, and we'd be ready to install some new occupants in no time. So, after a joint effort that liberated a surprising amount of richly-smelling old chicken shit from the house, an extensive de-spidering of the accommodation and a small amount of patching up, all that remained was to find some suitable hens. Maybe it was the time of year (early spring), or simply our ignorance, but neither newly hatched chicks, nor ready-to-lay pullets could be found. I never thought that there might be a shortage of chickens. This is green rural New Zealand, damn it. Come the start of November we were still without fowl, and the Waimate North Show was upon us. One of the best parts of the show, which deserves (and gets) a chapter all to itself, is the rare breed and small animals display. And there, amongst all the newborn lambs, the ducklings and piglets was a cage with four rather nondescript chicks. At last! We had found our hens. Then we had a good think; tiny chicks, cute but demonic cats, this might be a recipe for disaster (or at least a raw, feline delight). So we decided that, if we were to get some hens, they must be at least as large as the cats before we brought them home.

Thankfully, the lovely lady who bred chicks lived just up the road from us, and she was happy for us to buy them but not pick them up until January, when they'd be old enough to give an inquisitive cat a good peck. In the meantime, Laura became an online chicken expert, forearming herself with all the knowledge necessary to be a hen's best friend. We needed to find some sawdust, the ideal chicken bedding material. Just by chance, one of my patients was a worker at the steam sawmill, a working mill using ancient, steam powered equipment. We drove down to it, and not only were we allowed to help ourselves to huge bags of sawdust, we also had the rare and delightful privilege of leaping all over a newly piled huge pyramid of fresh sawdust to collect it. I would have loved this when I was seven. I loved it just as much now.

January arrived and off we went to Okaihau to pick up our brood. The farm was quite out of the way, and looked as if it had been established in the seventeenth century, which, of course, it wasn't. The pullets still seemed worryingly small but, with a thank-you and a gulp, we transferred them to one of the very useful boxes in which one of the cats had travelled from the UK, (with the help of an aeroplane) and off we went to show them their new home.

Back at the house, we released the chickens into their new, luxury accommodation and closed the door. The chicks followed us out of the coop, through a bigger-than-chick sized hole under the door. We led them back in, closed the door and placed a large log across the hole. The chicks followed us out through a slightly smaller hole under a laying stall. Eventually, and using the chicks as our testers, we rendered the hen house hen-proof. The pullets were a funny-looking flock, small and slightly wild looking, with inquisitive eyes and an inelegant gait. Our neighbour, Jean, came over to see them. She's an expert on poultry, and she thought they were a bit odd-looking too. She wasn't entirely sure that they any or all of them were females. Laura, however, had become fiercely proud of them within minutes of their arrival home. She was so sure that they were all female, that she named them accordingly; Millicent, Maude, Mabel and Matilda. After a week, the new occupants could be allowed the freedom of the chicken run. They were delighted! They disappeared into the long grass and bushes, and we thought we might never see them again.

Gradually, as the days went by, a routine became established. The growing pullets would appear and start to become noisy just when Laura was about to go and deliver some hen corn to them, or bring some scraps of food and egg shells from the kitchen. In places, the grass in the run became a little worn, but the chickens could still vanish into the undergrowth. And, in the spirit of 'The Ugly Duckling' these odd-looking pullets were developing into four very handsome shiny, green/black Menorca cross hens. By March we had decided to mow the grass in the hen run grass every so often, and the chickens seemed to really appreciate this, scrabbling through the new clippings for grubs and delighting in being able to run at full speed. And Laura`s instinct had once again been right for they had also started to lay eggs, not just any old eggs, but eggs with yolk so orange and tasty that scrambled, you would swear that I'd added saffron to the mixture. In time, we were getting four eggs every day, and we couldn't eat anywhere near their production! Our friends became the recipients of half-dozens at a time.

The chickens, being single minded, decided that roosting in the hen house was too soft for them and instead, started to roost in a small tree. This was a reasonable concept in midsummer, and escaped the heat of the night but the tree is a peach and loses its leaves in early autumn. Not a good wintery idea. And yet, even when they were sheltering from the most horrendous of storms during the day in the quiet comfort of the coop, they still insisted, come evening, on venturing out, and perching in the now wind-racked branches of the peach tree. Bird brains.

One day, in early October, Maude was in one of the laying stalls as usual, but whenever Laura went near her to collect eggs, she was greeted with an uncharacteristic hiss. Further approach was met with a determined peck, and no amount of persuasion could get her to leave the nest. At first, Laura was worried that Maude had become sick, but then we realised she had become broody. Of course, the eggs weren't fertile, so it was a wasted exercise. What was needed was some proper, vital eggs! Laura had been using an online forum called "Lifestyle block" and through that (how wonderful the internet can be!) she found a farmer in nearby Russell who was an expert in rare breeds of chickens. Sure enough, she had some eggs for sale, ready to be hatched. So off we went, and by that afternoon, Maude's broodiness was being channelled into useful activity. Meanwhile we had three weeks to build a broody house. With no design, no experience, two days later, we had a small, safe and warm mini hen house. We couldn't have been prouder! Of course, Laura had it painted a cute, cottagey pale blue in no time, and we moved Maude into her new residence, thus ensuring that, when the chicks (hopefully) were hatched, they would be protected from predators (including the other chickens), and especially the cats.

Three weeks later, to the day, the eggs started to hatch. We never saw the actual hatching as Maude, natural mother that she is, never moved from protecting them except for a little food and drink occasionally. So the first we knew of the new chicks was the characteristic weak "cheep" and a downy head, poking out from under Maude's breast feathers. In time there were five of these little heads and on closer inspection a day later, it was clear that the one remaining unhatched egg was not going to work. Later, in a piece of amateur dissection, we discovered that it had got really near the hatching stage, but then had died. So now we had five new chickens of indeterminate sex. Ideally, all five would have been hens.

Cockerels are handsome, huge and delicious, but Laura had banned me from even considering the possibility of killing and eating any of our adopted children, so we just had to hope that as many as possible would be female. By a quirk of nature, it seems that Laura is really good at determining the sex of chicks at a very early age.

"Three of them", she pronounced, "are hens, two are boys".

Normally, it's not possible to be sure of the chick's sex until they are about four to six weeks old, unless you look up the chick's "vent" and know what to look for when you get there. Laura does it by intuition. And it seems to work. So you might ask (if you knew) why the rooster is called Gladys. That seems like evidence of sexing gone awry. But no, there is a reason; Laura was so keen, when her sexing was done, to be wrong; that she named the rooster Gladys in the hope that, as he grew, he'd be so mortified by his name, that he'd become a hen. It didn't work. He took his styling cues from a packet of cornflakes, and hasn't looked back. He's a pure-bred New Hampshire Red rooster, and he's tall, elegant and has an absolutely classic crow that would wake the neighbours at five o`clock in the morning, were it not for the fact that the nearest neighbour is half a kilometre away!

We did, as you will have noticed, have another rooster, by the name of Bert. Bert was also a very handsome boy, but developed more slowly. We had high, optimistic hopes that the two of them would get on really well, but sadly, one day, we found them locked in serious combat, drawing blood from each other, and difficult to restrain. We had to separate them just to allow them to recover, and in the end we were grateful that we could find a suitable home for Bert before he became mortally bullied. The other three chickens are now beautiful proud hens, and laying eggs, huge brown eggs. Sensibly, they gave up roosting in the nearly bare peach tree next to the Menorcas. Perhaps they noticed that it rains there more than it does in the hen house, or perhaps they're made of softer stuff than the wiry older hens, but they now overnight indoors, because they are just as clever as they need to be.

Watching chickens is more rewarding than most people imagine. The interaction, inquisitiveness and enthusiasm that they display, and their lack of timidity make them every bit as interesting as any other creature that we get to watch up close. Think of it as a safari in the garden. All the excitement of the chase for food, the pack behaviour, the henpecking, and even the sexual politics are exhibited. And as if it was not enough that they entertain us in this way, and give us a way to dispose of all our food scraps sensibly, they also provide us with the most amazing eggs. They delight us with their antics and their eggs, we delight them with their safe, secure home and an endless supply of food.

Hello, Ducks!

Ducks are entertaining, noisy, dirty, smelly and funny. I'm sure that reminds me of someone I know, but I can't work out who it is. Laura decided that her next foray into the world of poultry should be duck based and a friend of hers, who is a breeder of rare poultry, had some Silver Appleyard ducks for sale. They were only three weeks old, so I had visions of furry little chicks peeping and running around. Not a bit of it. At three weeks they are nearly full grown.

We brought seven ducks home, or to be more precise, four ducks and three drakes, and within a few weeks, as winter came to an end, it became apparent that this was too many drakes for the ladies. The males initially squabbled for superiority, but having established a ruthless pecking order, they proceeded to bully the females in a way that can only be described as rape. It's not a pretty sight to see the violence with which these funny and handsome animals force themselves on their slightly drab-looking mates.

Meanwhile, despite the fact that they were flightless, the territory claimed by the ducks as they free ranged the farm expanded, especially when they discovered the stream. They always came back morning and night with the hope of a corn feed to supplement their insect and slug diet. And their egg laying was as random as their foraging. We found eggs in the paddocks, eggs under trees, and even eggs in the little wooden box in which we transported them. Before too long, the females started to take time out from their busy schedule of quacking, foraging and being attacked to go broody, one at a time. They chose the most protected place they could find, a big pile of wood that was supposed to be a winter bonfire, and ensconced themselves so deeply in the woodpile that we had no option but to wait for the ducklings to hatch before we decided what to do next. The first brood hatched and we caught them in a rare moment when the female let her guard down (otherwise she rushed her brood deep into the woodpile) and moved them out of the reach of the harriers that circle overhead looking for Silver Appleyard ducklings. So they went into the broody house that Laura and I had built in another chapter and, three weeks later, could leave as they were almost fully grown. By the time they all hatched, we would have a breeding population of approximately three million ducks, and, whilst the breed is famously good as a roast (as well as a good egg layers) I was under strict instructions that all ducks are to stay alive. If surplus to requirements, then Wayne and Millie's daughter, Anna had first dibs on them, and they will populate her pond. Now, I wonder if I should suggest to

Laura that goose eggs are very good for baking...

Rachel, Joseph & Sheba

When I was young and growing up in the Yorkshire Dales, for a few years we had donkeys as pets, living in a small paddock behind the garden. So, in my pastoral haze, I felt that our new home would be enhanced by some donkey guests. We contacted the local donkey organisations and asked if they knew any for sale. We found out that, despite the donkey being little more than a pet in New Zealand, few are available for sale. They are rarely used for any agricultural duties, although a stallion or "jack" might be used to keep bulls well behaved. Then we saw an advert placed on the notice board of the local supermarket looking for a new home for a couple of elderly, well-mannered donkeys.

Donkeys live to a good old age. Many can reach forty years, and beyond in exceptional cases - I have read that the record is fifty five - so when I heard that these two, called Rachel and Joseph, were in their early thirties, I wasn't too concerned. We went to see them, and I was instantly captivated. Joseph was unusual for a jack, being placid and friendly, slightly knock-kneed and smaller than his lifelong partner who was tall and stately and a little aloof. They lived on the other side of Kerikeri, and their owners, who had looked after them since they were foals, brought them over in a horse float a few days later. We already had a paddock ideal for their needs with little stables and plenty of shelter, and they settled in very quickly. Joseph was quite randy, and pursued Rachel around the paddock, braying noisily and ignoring any suggestions from her that the dozen or so foals they had already raised were quite enough, thanks.

Because donkeys originate in the Middle East and North Africa, where their usual diet is scrubby bushes, we had to make their paddock quite small and keep a keen eye out for signs of over-eating which, in turn can lead to severe problems with their feet. By a stroke of luck, our neighbour behind the farm is a farrier, and he came over every three months or so to trim their hooves, a process that they both were familiar with and grateful for. They thrived, with daily visits from us bearing wee gifts of fresh veggies, and plenty of visitors to give them all the attention they needed.

In time, there was the occasional moment when, by introducing them to the bulls we had on the property, it was clear that they would be a controlling influence if necessary, although it never came to that. They are fearless! But gradually, we came to experience the slow sadness that comes with the burden of years. Joseph, always the dominant one of the pair, took a blow to the face (we think his amorous advances may have resulted in a swift kick) and he was very sorry for himself. His demeanour suddenly altered, he began to be withdrawn and silent, his coat became matt and rough and he started to lose weight.

Suddenly he wouldn't approach us, was nervous of the farrier and wasn't eating nearly enough. Blood tests showed that physically he was well, he was just an old man. We kept him as comfortable as possible, but Rachel, who was sleek and pretty as ever, seemed to revel in his misfortune. She was now the one that brayed for attention and rushed forward for any treats. Nature and time can be so cruel. We looked at Joseph on a daily basis and wondered if we were prolonging the cruelty by letting him slowly fade. I didn't want to play god, but neither did I want him to suffer. For a while he wandered the paddock, the very embodiment of Eeyore. I knew that we would know when the time had come. So sad and yet, how odd it is that we know what is right for the beasts in our care, but we cannot extend this humanity to humans. We truly are an odd bunch of apes.

Inevitably, this gradual degeneration continued and Joseph became completely blind. When he walked into an electric fence and couldn't extricate himself from it without our help, we knew that he had little time left and called the vet for advice. Further tests painted a sad picture, and alas, our grey old gentleman is no more. We were sadder than we expected. We knew that this would happen one day, but his absence was quite palpable. Rachel seemed to be more aware of him in death than she did in life, wandering along the periphery, braying, then suddenly running the length of the paddock, and then stopping, as if confused by her turn of speed.

Donkeys, especially those used to company, do not thrive on solitude, and before long we found out that a friend of ours, a local nurse, had a donkey, Sheba, looking for a new home. Sheba was no stranger to our place. She'd been introduced to Joseph not long after we first brought our donkeys home, in the hope that she might bear a foal. No chance! In the three months that she was with us, it had been necessary to keep her and Joseph apart as they were incompatible. Joseph was not the issue, he was very keen for Sheba to become pregnant. But Sheba not only refused to come into season, she also developed a kung-fu like turn of speed and kicking ability. Joseph was not deterred, so was put in another paddock for his own protection.

So Sheba returned to the farm, slender but rather bedraggled, wearing her winter coat well into the summer, then losing it in great clumps. The sudden glut of grass was too much for her self control and within weeks she had become so rotund that we halved the size of the paddock while she was still able to walk. Thankfully she and Rachel get on well together, wandering around their mini-paddock in tandem, lonesome no more and very noisy if there is even the slightest chance of some feed coming their way.

The Rise of the Alpacas

I often drove past farms with paddocks in which funny looking, long necked animals were grazing. In the winter, they looked like a cross between a teddy bear and a giraffe and in the summer, freshly sheared, they shrank to comical spindly mini-Llamas. Alpacas are becoming popular in New Zealand, and it's not hard to see why. Laura shared my delight in seeing these little woolly beasts, and we had often discussed what it might be like to keep them.

Meanwhile... our steers, having been looked after by us for nearly two years, had become huge! They were still as friendly as ever, galloping over at high speed if there was any possibility of a trough of molasses-rich feed, or even a good forehead scratch! This friendliness was not unwelcome, but was becoming a little unnerving, so clearly it was time to look at selling them on and starting from the beginning again. We contacted James, our friendly, helpful stock agent (yet another connection I can assure you I had never envisaged having in my now ever-fading memory of urban life!) and we arranged for our bovine friends to be collected. A week later a huge cattle truck appeared in the drive and inched its way into the stockyards. The drive was overgrown and only just wide enough for the lorry. The driver, however, was the epitome of calm, so I suspect that we're probably not the only small farm with a tiny drive. He backed the truck up to the loading ramp and the steers needed only the slightest encouragement to get on. In fact, the driver, who usually had to use a cattle-prod, was most impressed with their affability. I hope this reflected well on our attempt to give these animals the best possible life before they return the favour with their beef. The news from the stockyards was good; the price is set internationally, and was very high. We had raised some animals that were well appreciated by beef finishing farmers, and they went to be given a final over-winter fattening before their final journey to an abattoir.

This makes us sad if we dwell on it but, as meat eaters, we also are well aware of the potential for hypocrisy. Knowing that the beasts had a wonderful life, and knowing that this meant they would make the best quality beef, we dwelt on this thought rather than the painful reality of their death, and the circuit was closed. We should feel some sadness. That's proof that we're not psychopaths. So, for the first time in ages, we switched off the electric fence, and in midwinter the paddocks were bare, the grass rested, and the farm was quiet. Except for Sheba; she just needed to see me and she brayed like a mad-ass.

By late spring, the grass (and the thistles, and the carrot weed, and the dock) in the paddocks was going crazy.

James had promised that as soon as he found some really quiet, happy, docile weaner steers he'd let us know, but nothing seemed to be happening. We were getting a little worried that our beautiful, orderly pasture was becoming a derelict and overgrown mess, so good old Billy the Tractor was brought out of semi-retirement, fired up (with a jumpstart) and filled with diesel. The slasher was attached and off Laura went, 'topping off' the paddocks to control the weeds before they flowered. She soon discovered that the wind-borne chaff from all the mowing was a bit irritating. She came inside after an evening of mowing a meadow with her eyes barely open, reddened and weepy; by the morning it looked as if she'd been in a fight, so dark were the circles. The next time she went slashing, she wore a scuba diving mask. It might have looked comical, but it worked a treat!

One evening, as we were sitting down to our supper, a cattle truck appeared in the gloaming. And the drive. We initially assumed that the friendly Hilder's driver had got the wrong farm, but no, it was eleven steer weaners with our name on them. Not literally, we don't approve of branding. But there they were, docile, cute, skinny and pale, Charolais cross calves, all of twelve weeks old. We put them into a small paddock where they wandered, a little dazed, and then settled and slept. The next morning, we let them into a bigger paddock that Laura had slashed, where they frolicked and ate to capacity, with bulging tummies. I turned the electric fence back on. Their tummies clearly weren't bulging enough. Within a week they had started to look further afield for their grazing, and further meant the neighbour's garden. I couldn't understand it. The fence they walked through was seven wires, in good condition and electrified. I checked the electric fence yet again, drove in more earth stakes (add that to my list of things I never thought I'd ever do) tightened the fence wires, yet still they seemed convinced that the grass, lush though ours might be, was greener on the other side. We moved them to more secure paddocks away from our market-gardening neighbour. They ate all the grass. We moved them back. They pushed through again. After four weeks of this, we were getting more than a little stressed.

"James, what do you think we should do? We really like the steers, they're ideal for us, but they won't stay in the paddock we put them in." I asked.

"Once they start pushing through, they'll keep the habit. I'd sell them on if I were you," was James's advice.

So we did. The steers went back to the market and sold the next day.

Although Laura was little wary of the idea, we kept one steer to fatten up for our freezer (it would be the prettiest one, with a heart-shaped blaze, that she named

Sweetheart), one that never wandered, so we thought we could trust it. But what would we do with the farm? We could go back to renting the pasture to another farmer, but we weren't keen on that option after our newly-acquired expertise. We could have the paddocks cut for hay; it was fetching a good price in the winter, and we may well do that with some of the acreage, but our mind drifted to alpacas, and lodged there. A nearby farm breeds them, and they're not cheap, but they are intriguing. We went and had a look at them up close. We researched their care, their habits, their needs, and we suddenly found ourselves the proud owners of three handsome males who, by sheer coincidence, were roughly the same colours as our dogs. These animals were an absolute delight! After starting out a little aloof and nervous, they became, in varying degrees, affectionate, trusting, and relaxed. One of them, Darjeeling, was the boss, and he was rather wary of us, dictating his terms to the others by spitting (but never at us, I'm delighted to report; the phlegm stinks and has a local anaesthetic effect, apparently). The other two boys, Tetley and Earl Grey, were much more trusting, would eat out of our hand, liked being stroked, and made bizarre and appealing conversational grunts when in our presence.

Alpacas do need some care. Every three months or so, their huge, claw-like toenails need a trim, and every year their extraordinary fleece needs shearing. The wool, finer even than Merino, is highly prized, and produced prolifically.

Getting wool off the alpacas was interesting. They were too big, too wriggly and too independent to allow a shearer to treat them like a sheep. And so Ray arrived (invited, of course) with a shearing table. Ray was (and still is) a champion sheep shearer, which is saying something in New Zealand, and he had recently turned his hand to alpaca shearing, realising that the popularity of this odd animal was rising. He set up his gear in a stock pen; the table, about the size of a pool table, was vertical, more like a wall. He grabbed the first alpaca, Tetley and, while I held him and made what I hoped were reassuring noises, Ray pressed him against the table and put a big velcro strap round his middle. Once secure, Tetley calmed down and allowed Ray to tie off his legs so that the big strap could be released. Then the table was laid horizontal at waist height, and the shearing could start. About five minutes later, the job was done, the wool collected and Tetley was released looking comically striped, shaved (except for the sunburn vulnerable head and ears) and shrunken. Ray was very swift, very accurate, and although a man of few words, a great demonstrator of the art of shearing, yet very gentle with these potentially skittish animals. Only Darjeeling complained about the process, with a high, mournful and rather human howl, which, much to my surprise, made the other two run over to him, touch noses, and look quite concerned. Tetley even gathered Darjeeling's wool into a pile and curled up in it, sniffing it all the while. We thought the two subservient animals would delight in their dominant brother's discomfort, but it was quite the opposite. Ray, who had a huge amount of experience with these creatures, said that, in common with other gregarious animals, being the alpha is a stressful role, and not one of control so much as responsibility. We all pondered on that over a cup of tea. Tetley for the men, Earl Grey for Laura.

Whilst they are long lived and hardy, one disease alpacas are prone to is facial eczema. This is caused by a fungus that grows on leaf mould, and the spores that can proliferate in warm humid weather can get into the blood of the animal, and cause liver failure and death. The breaking of blood vessels that the spores cause is most visible on the face of the sufferer, hence the name. To treat this disease is very difficult, so prevention is the best option. Keeping leaf mould to a minimum is a good idea, so we never slashed the paddock the alpacas frequent. We separated them from the donkeys, despite the fact that they all got on really well together, because it was discovered a few years ago (by a dental nurse) that zinc supplement to their diet seems to reduce the incidence of the disease. Although this is still controversial, it does mean that we can't feed the animals together. Rachel and Sheba are far too strong, wily and above all, greedy to give the alpacas the chance to feed alongside them. So the three of them have their own paddock, and know their feeding trough. They glide over in that effortless way that they run, at the slightest chance of some zinc-laced food.

The rise continues

Down the road is the Alpaca farm from whence came the 3 boys who now live with us. We've had them for about 9 months, and they have been a delight to care for, so, a few weeks ago, with money saved from the sale of the wayward steers, we selected 3 females, all of them pregnant (we hoped) by a stud male of excellent pedigree. One of them, Vienna, is older (about 9) and the mother of Tetley, our friendliest male. We could instantly see where he gets his affable temperament from; she is calm, small, dark-coated and bewhiskered. Very cute. The other two, Cocoa and Truffle are younger, bigger, and a bit more aloof, but all of them have a grace that sets them apart from the male adolescents in the paddock next door.

Alpaca gestation is a variable occurrence. Usually set at eleven and a half months, it can be a good four weeks either way. The females "choose" their delivery day depending on the weather, the presence of predators and, for all I know, the numerological significance of the date. One morning, Laura was down at the cottage, cleaning it after the departure of the recent guests when she noticed a plastic carrier bag in the alpacas' paddock. She wandered over to remove it before they had a chance to chew on it, when it sprang up, and bounced away. No ordinary carrier bag; this was Herbert (or Herbie) and he was, at a few hours old, our first cria (the technical term for a baby alpaca). He was born without fuss, healthy, happy, and, with a quick weigh to check that he wasn't too premature, and a little help to remove the quick-setting plasticky remains of the amniotic sac that had dried around his neck, he was ready to spring and bound all over the paddock. Oddly enough, what with him being Vienna's cria, he is very pale. His ears were folded at a comical angle, which is normal for a premature cria, and he was tiny and shivering, so we ordered him a waterproof coat, he grew fast and healthy, and before long, the only thing he needed was a friend to play with. He was jumping on the backs of his aunties and his mum, so it was with some delight and relief that, just a few weeks later, Stella was born. Whereas Herbie is stocky, blunt and demanding, Stella is a leggy, delicate and more faun-like creature. She was born just before we saw her, still wet and shivering, unable to stand, and very thin. We worried for her; the weather had just taken a turn for the unpleasant, with days of rain forecast, and cold nights for the first time in ages.

We went off to get Herbie's old coat (cleaned of his smell, of course) and when we got back to the paddock, only 30 minutes later, she was gone. With some concern we walked to the other side of the paddock (down a shallow hill) and along came all the alpacas, at a graceful trot hoping for some of their dried food. Stella, at the tender age of one hour, was already running! It makes sense that herbivores, especially gregarious ones, must be able to get mobile that fast or be eaten. She was being pestered by Herbie who wanted to play and wouldn't let her anywhere near Cocoa, her mum, so we scooped her up, rubbed the coat on her to imbue it with her scent, put it on her and put her and Cocoa into one of the yards, away from Herbie's unwanted attention.

It was clear that she was going to be more high-maintenance than her cousin when we noticed that her attempts to suckle weren't working. The first 3 days of a cria's life are absolutely dependent on the colostrum in the first milk that they get from their mum, and if she didn't feed she wouldn't survive. We phoned Alex and Janet who live a few kilometers away and from whom we bought our beasts, and they came over to have a look and offer advice. They suggested we make up some colostrum from powder and bottle-feed Stella, and so we did, feeling all down to earth and farmy. She didn't take to the bottle feeding so well, and whenever I went near her, Cocoa's usual conversational humming would turn into bleats of alarm and concern, and she'd use her powerful neck to push me out of the way. So Laura coo'd in her ear and gently held her back as I attempted to administer the warm, rich milk (which is packed with immunoglobulins, and the only defence the new cria has against infections), and indeed, she did drink some. And the rest went down my arm.

Releasing her, she immediately went to Cocoa's udders, and gradually, she gave us a reasonable demonstration of the art of suckling as if to say "this is what you're trying to show me, isn't it?". But she seemed so small, so shivery, and spindly that we worried about her all the same.

The next morning, we got up and went to the yard, and, despite the rain and cold, she was there, feeding and sheltering under Cocoa. We weighed her, to her mum's renewed consternation (I stand on the scales, weigh myself, Laura passes me Stella, and we subtract my weight from the total) and our relief; she's put on a few hundred grammes. Because the weather had become so wet, we decided to let her and Cocoa back with the herd, and they all ran off to the far side of the paddock where there is more shelter. Again, all Herbie wants to do is play, play, play.

Travelling South

The only time we ever want to leave Northland is in the winter. When the days shorten and the rain falls more often than not, it's time to get away, Usually we pick somewhere hot and exotic such as the tropical islands of the Pacific. But one year we decided to take our holiday in late autumn, and go and see the South Island. Or the mainland, as the locals call it.

Before we left Scotland, more than a few people expressed surprise at our choice of Northland as our destination. They had heard that the South Island, and especially Christchurch, was the place to be, with impressive scenery, low population, and an almost "1950s in Britain" feel. It sounded to them like civilized paradise and, for many, perhaps it is. But, coming from Scotland, we really didn't want to move to somewhere that, despite its antipodean location, was so similar to the place we'd left behind. I mean, Dunedin is the Gallic for Edinburgh!

However, we did want to see what we were missing. So, after a morale plummeting evening with some friends of friends who assured us with some confidence that we were going to spend the entire month in cold, rain and snow, we set off in the trusty Subaru, leaving our farm in the care of a couple of good pals. We drove to Auckland, a familiar drive by now, and then beyond, into unknown territory. Hours later (about eleven of them) we had traversed the whole of the North Island in one easy step. The roads were good and swift, the scenery varied and dramatic and the occasional stops for coffee and the odd sandwich or pie, varied and undramatic.

Wellington was a brief blur. We arrived quite late, checked into a serviced apartment for the night, and went in search of good food. I was happy to walk until we found something suitable. Laura, who was very tired, really just wanted a simple, quick meal before bedtime. Naturally, neither of us got our wish. What we thought was going to be a very short walk just dragged on, the restaurant was fully booked and the taxi driver we eventually stopped had difficulty understanding us. Perhaps we were less intelligible than we thought, or perhaps he was as tired as we were! Eventually we did find somewhere to eat, then back to the apartment to sleep and get up early enough to catch the Inter-Islander ferry to Picton on a calm, sunny and life-affirming morning.

And suddenly, we were in the South Island. So, in holiday mood, we sped southwards, heading for Kaikoura through the rolling, vine-rich hills of Marlborough. Because it was mid-May, Kaikoura was nearly closed. We found a helpful and comfortable little motel in which we had the run of the place and they arranged our first foray into arch-tourism, the whale watching for which this tiny town is well known. For me, this was a return to an activity that had been the highlight of my previous visit to the South Island a mere eighteen years previously. Back then, a dozen of us had been whisked out into the suddenly very deep sea by a crew of extremely enthusiastic marine environmentalists in a high-speed RIB. We got soaked by the spray, but so close to a sperm whale called Hoon that we could smell his rank, rotten-squid breath. When he slapped his tail fluke before submerging, we applauded, and then we were soaked again. Eighteen years later, everything was very different. The trip out to sea was preceded by a lesson about whales and their habitat before boarding a very flash, purpose built catamaran with comfy seats, video screens and no exposure to the elements (even if we wanted it). With food and drink available, no buffeting from the waves, and the ever present drip-feed of valuable information, we were in a floating classroom with a cetacean theme. The hunt for the whales was just the same as it was all those years ago, using hydrophones to locate the chattering behemoths, but there was a distance that we never closed when we encountered one. So is this progress, or not? I felt like a character from a certain book by Melville.

“Back in the days of yore, you could smell their stinking breath” I muttered.

But who cared? The new, remote, almost virtual way of whale watching is the only way now. And perhaps more respect is given to the needs of the whales, free from the prying eyes of daily tourists. I preferred the old way (what, could you guess?) but I suspect that it won't return. That night we took a stroll along the sea front for about ten seconds. Then I sprinted back, grabbed the car and we drove along the sea front; it was blowing a gale, and freezing. We were certainly south now. And the fish and chips were very good.

We'd arranged to meet up, and stay with a family in Christchurch with whom Laura and I had "spoken" for ages through an internet forum. They too had recently migrated to New Zealand and had made their home in Canterbury. Nobody at this time had the slightest intimation that this was a land with poor foundations. Christchurch was a bit of a disappointment for us. I say this after the earthquakes with a pang of guilt. At the time, we had no reason to feel sorry for the Cathedral City, but even in clear sunny weather it seemed grey and soulless, a bit seedy, and not very friendly. We were clearly unlucky in that regard, but we can't change the past. Our friends with whom we stayed were lovely, a warm and boozy family who made us laugh and feel instantly welcome, but the city still felt charmless. Now, Christchurch is a city with special needs and it would probably be seen as politically incorrect to criticise. We really wanted to like it more, but we breathed a mutual sigh of relief that we had decided, entirely on intuition, that our friends back in the "old country" had been wrong to recommend Canterbury to us as our destination before we migrated.

Onwards and upwards, this time to Arrowtown. We'd booked in for a few nights here, as we were both looking forward to its quaint, rural, alpine appeal. We weren't disappointed. If it was any more quaint, it might feel as if it had been built by Disney but, as an antidote to that, it's only thirty minutes away from Queenstown, the adrenaline-fuelled heart of modern New Zealand. So we dotted between the two, eating well, sampling the Central Otago produce (especially the Pinot Noir), and scaring ourselves silly on the Shotover Jet boat.

Te Anau is a pretty, quiet town on the lakeside. We'd heard plenty about it from our well-travelled friends and were looking forward to some time to relax, look around and try out some of the more touristy activities, especially a trip to Fjordland. By now, it was so out of season that we felt as if we had the run of the place, so we had a look at the grander, well established hotels on the lakefront. The first one we looked at had impressive signs extolling their huge rooms, great breakfasts and free wifi access, but, on closer inspection (when we looked at the room) it had the atmosphere of a morgue and the smell of an old damp tarpaulin. We beat a retreat. We then decided to throw caution to the wind and try a very opulent looking place. The receptionist seemed amazed (and delighted) to see us. The hotel was being renovated, all the older rooms were very cheap but the newer, recently redecorated ones were too, and turned out to be very luxurious. So that's where we stopped - five star luxury, on the lakeside, and almost the whole place to ourselves. We spent a few days there as a base, enjoying wonderful hospitality and the excellent little bar restaurants.

We had a really superb trip to and upon Milford Sound, taking a small four wheel drive bus in which we were the only occupants, and a helicopter ride onto a nearby glacier. This I enjoyed greatly but Laura spent the entire trip, including the glacier stop, in a perpetual state of near panic. She did very well to hold on, the only external indication that she wasn't having the time of her life was a rather fixed grin and one, solitary tear running down her cheek. We were very sad to leave Te Anau, and will certainly return.

We started to move north again, this time, briefly, to Wanaka, a very lovely town, quite modern, very affluent, (or so it felt after Te Anau) and serving excellent coffee. Our next destination was the west coast, so we moved on, and found ourselves in the rugged west, at Franz Josef. Franz Josef is a town that thrives on tourism, and the focus for visitors is the glacier that sits behind it, tumbling imperceptibly down the mountains and beckoning the ice-loving tourists. I was keen to do a little climbing on this frozen monument, and signed up for an all day walk with one of the travel companies. The next morning, very early, I found myself getting measured up for stout boots, crampons and an ice-axe. And surrounded by a busload of enthusiastic tourists all young enough to be my children. Even our guides were young, hyper fit twenty-somethings. I started to suspect that the "suitable for all ages and levels of fitness" description of the day might be of little relevance in the face of such youthful exuberance. A short bus journey and a slightly longer walk to the base of the glacier brought us to a point where it was clear on closer inspection that the glacier, so pristine and benign when viewed from a distance, was really menacing, crumbly and dirty at its foot. We were given instructions on how to put on the crampons, how to use an ice-axe, and a safety briefing. We then split up into various groups determined by speed and enthusiasm, and, it would seem, age. As the oldest person there, I was put in the fastest group. No idea why. Maybe they thought I had more experience with putting one foot in front of the other, in the time honoured tradition. So off we went, carefully threading our way up the ice which, we quickly discovered, is as hard as rock and as abrasive as a cheese grater, especially if you fall.

Getting used to the crampons was tricky at first but, as with so many aspects of hill walking, once a rhythm is established, it just flows (what an odd word is rhythm...). Before long, the base of the glacier was well below us, and the ice was looking pristine, wet and blue, transparent and beguiling and I was entranced, lost in the cadence of my steps, my breath, and the near silence of the glacier (apart from the occasional youthful outpouring of expletives). We climbed high up on ice, pausing briefly, traversing impossibly narrow ledges (those crampons are amazing once you start to trust them), ascending impossibly beautiful tunnels of ice, and marvelling that, within a couple of days, the entire topography will have become rearranged. By mid-afternoon, the sunshine had got to work on the ice, and rivulets of meltwater could be seen and heard under the surface, which had become slick and treacherous. Our guide decided to bring us downwards again.

Not surprisingly, going down a glacier is much harder than going up. Gravity seems determined to turn a controlled walk into a precipitous rush, and suddenly we became aware of how high we had climbed, and how shaky our knees had become. But again, a pattern becomes established, and we descended quite quickly. I was starting to feel quite cold towards the base of the glacier, and passed up on an opportunity to take all my clothes off and have a swim in an ice-hole, (yes, I will use that word). Before long, and just before sunset, we were walking, crampon-free, back to the bus. The walk out seemed miles longer than the walk in. I was more exhausted than I have ever been. I even hit "the wall" on that last little walk, when I really thought I could walk no further, but a robust mental attitude (or maybe the bloke behind barging into me as I stopped unexpectedly) forced me on. Relieved to be back at the bus, our guide told me that was the highest he had ever taken a walking group up the glacier. The weather had been perfect, and the party young and agile enough to make good progress. Then I didn't feel quite so exhausted. In fact I was so buoyed up with elation that I nearly ran back to the motel after we were dropped off in town. I don't remember anything more that evening. We may well have eaten, and slept, but it's a blank.

The west coast of the South Island is stunning. Huge native beech forests give way to rugged, big-pebbled beaches, cliffs and coves, with hardly any sign of human habitation. It's the kind of landscape that ensures the few people who grow up there feel out of place anywhere else, and these "coasters" as they are called are proud of their heritage. Following the Buller river inland, we suddenly reached Nelson. So suddenly that we had two days in hand. And what a pleasant surprise that was. Nelson is one of those "Goldilocks" towns, big enough to have a bustling and fashionable market, small enough to walk around in an afternoon. We loved the place and agreed that, if we hadn't put down such deep roots so quickly and fallen for Northland so hard, Nelson would have been our next best choice for a place to live in New Zealand.

After a weekend in Nelson, enjoying some sightseeing in the company of two friends we caught up with there, and favouring various restaurants and bars with our presence, it was time for us to return home. Sadly, our holiday was over. We drove north almost as swiftly as we did south, revelling in the weeks of beauty, majesty and sunshine that we had just enjoyed, unaware that, for the next three months in Northland, the sun would barely show its face, nor would the rain cease. But we kept ourselves warm with the visions of the south. And most of our store of firewood.

The Meaning of Life?

In my experience, books that tell the story of a change in lifestyle and habit, always reach a point where physical description is replaced by philosophical discourse. If you, as the avid reader (and, thanks for that, by the way, you have remarkable taste, extraordinary stamina, and by default, are beautiful, witty and wise.) know what I am alluding to, and loathe it, then remove the next chapter from your copy of the book. I have arranged with the publishers for the next three pages to be cunningly perforated so that modification of this book to suit your tastes can be achieved with ease. The publisher, in turn, has suggested that the whole book may be perforated in just such a way so that it may all be binned the moment after you buy it, thus cutting out the middle man, and classifying the book as a "labour-saving device with a negative carbon footprint".

I'm back on track and was about to write about contentment. I'm in my mid-forties. It wasn't always thus, and will only remain so for a couple more years and, with the dawning of what used to be called middle age, comes the potential for a measure of self-understanding. In the last few years I have come to the conclusion that the holy grail of my youthful life, the quest for happiness, was an illusion. That's not to say I wasn't happy, but it is to say that I didn't create the happiness. Here's the notion, and please forgive me if you read what I am saying and start to make Valley-Girl sarcastic noises because it was all so obvious to your Mensa-defining intellect (in which case you probably hate this book anyway). If ever you wondered, I have always preferred "hello" to be a jovial greeting, not a rude and sarcastic question. (You do know what I'm talking about here, don't you? The rise of the sarcastic "hello?" is one of my pet hates. Pretty soon, if I keep this up, I'll become one of yours). Happiness is an emotional state and can only exist in close collaboration with sadness, its nemesis. Wanting to be happy, as an ambition, is seriously flawed in this respect. The happiness you will enjoy will only ever be as intense as the sadness with which it alternates. Purveyors of things, whether it is the new car, the lovely home, or even this book, cannot guarantee happiness, but they might promise to. And that's the catch. Yes, seeing your shiny new car sitting on your beautiful drive framed by the delightful curtains of your lovely home may well create an upwelling of happy feelings. You may well have easily enough funds in your bank account that the car, drive, home and curtains are all paid for, but that happiness is fleeting and a result of you being human and flawed, and not some cosmic payback for all the work you have done (as we are so often led to believe). In fact, if you have paid for them all, they may make you less happy, as they may be belittled by the ease with which they were achieved. But here we are, talking about the effect that possessions have on our emotional state. (well I am, you're listening, or quietly tearing the oh so useful perforated pages) But it's not just possessions, it's everything. Relationships, food, the view, air quality, belief in the sanctity of the baby Jesus, and his dad, God.

Anything that attempts to distract you from what is important to you is an illusion, and that includes Buddhism, (just in case any of you Buddhists were anticipating a lovely view from the existential high ground). No! The real secret of life, the unemotional trick that you have to pull on your mind is contentment. If you can look at any beautiful house, view, car, holiday, curtains without a pang of desire (or worse, jealousy) then you are in fine mental shape, and possibly not entirely human. However, it really is a state of mind in which you are likely to enjoy life more than you would by going down the other path. That's the one where the advertising works, the constant mindset is that of acquisition and nothing achieved is ever enough. That way you get your share of happiness and sadness, but your contentment quota will be seriously lacking.

Now, I suspect that there may be those amongst you who wonder how in hell I have the nerve to preach contentment when I have so many possessions myself (OK, I'm projecting a bit here, I don't know you anywhere nearly as well as you know me). There is an element of preaching in the last few paragraphs, and I apologise. The reason that I can say all this stuff with such barefaced cheek is that I'm human, and we do things like that. Yes it's annoying, and I like it no more than anyone else but, despite that fact, this is not an argument, It's my book, my opinion. I am, in this microcosm, right and that's what matters.

So what's so good about being content? Doesn't it sound a bit god-bothery? A bit lacking in ambition? This is the paradox. Hold on tight, because here comes the secret of life: Happiness is always tempered by subsequent sadness (the vice-versa is also true, for all you nihilists). But, with the attainment of contentment, where wanting or needing is banished, then happiness can exist without it's opposite. This is a state of grace, and only exists for as long as the contentment does, but when you know yourself really well, these moments can be stretched to encompass as much as, ooh, a whole second. Actually, I'm pretty new to this, but I reckon that if you're really honest with yourself, life could be made up of such moments. I'm not suggesting that you divest yourself of all trappings of success, just those elements of your life you have been talked into by peer pressure, whether it's advertising, friends, religion or nationalism. They're all made up, and if they don't fit your self-understanding, they should go. If I hadn't already made this clear, the whole reason that I've inserted this chapter into an otherwise optimistic and bucolic tale of migration and self-discovery is that, without the realisation that happiness was not the defining quality for which I was searching, I may never have felt the urge to stop digging the hole in which I was standing. Patronising rant over. No harm done. It's all good.

Classic Car Behaviour

When I was young, in the days when there were no laws governing the use of car seatbelts, My dad had a Mk2 Jaguar. If you watch any film or TV programme involving a crime in the 1960s, it's the one used as a getaway car. It was, in my memory, classy, fast and luxurious. He's had all sorts of motors since then, but that Jag was always the one that stuck in my mind. So when a good example of its sister car, the Daimler 250 came up for sale locally, impetuously, I bought it. It was in fine shape apart from a few minor niggles, it drove well, looked and felt great. Of course, being over forty years old, it was a little idiosyncratic, but nothing I couldn't take care of. I joined classic car clubs, we took it on slow sunday drives with like-minded enthusiasts, and I turned a blind eye to its constant and expensive demands.

The police in New Zealand pay a good deal of attention to the prevention and detection of drunken driving. Around holiday time, this includes setting up temporary roadblocks and checking everybody's breath for alcohol in a very rapid, efficient and perfunctory way. And whilst I agree that no one should drive whilst intoxicated, I have, on occasion, had a glass of wine with a meal before driving home. Just the one. Really.

On one particular occasion, Laura, her Mum and I had been out for a meal and, just as I pulled into the petrol station for a fill-up, I noticed the characteristic crowd of cars that accompanies the police booze-check. So, since she hadn't drunk anything, I suggested that Laura take over the driving. This was the first time she had driven the Daimler, and was not necessarily the best introduction to vintage motoring. The Daimler has no power steering, so turning at slow speeds requires shoulder strength. That's no big deal but, for reasons I hadn't been able to fathom, leaning on the wheel set off the horn. The engine was running a little rich, and prone to stalling and backfiring. Oh, and the gear selector is on the steering column, where you would, in a modern car, find the indicator stalk.

Laura drove up to the roadblock, announcing her presence with the eccentric use of horn, stopped as requested, whereupon the car backfired twice then stalled. The policeman checked her breath, which was fine. Laura tried to start the engine again, it backfired, she put the car into reverse, nearly colliding with the car behind us, it backfired, stalled, restarted and then lurched off, sounding the horn again a couple of times for good measure. When she stalled again, another policeman, slightly the worse for his mirth, asked if she wouldn't mind repeating the breath test as the other machine was obviously faulty. We eventually got underway again, wheezing and staggering up the road with no good measure of the usual grace I associate with those beautiful cars.

Eventually the Daimler ran nicely, and I put it up for sale. It was the most beautiful, irritating, wonderful, nostalgic money pit I've ever had! Any takers?

Evenings on the beach

Our friends Millie and Wayne have the good fortune to own, on their property, a lovely, tiny, pohutukawa-lined cove. The pohutukawa is a stunning, evergreen tree, a well-loved native of northern New Zealand, which flowers in an extravagant crimson display around Christmas time. New Zealanders generally regard it as their "Christmas tree" and around midsummer the traditional cards will portray a Pohutukawa flower, sometimes with a dusting of snow, for irony, and in deference to the ancestry of the festival.

On a small hillock within this cove, sheltered from the breezes, stands a small old fashioned wooden beach hut. This is Crayfish Cottage, and it has become the kitchen for regular, yet impromptu feasts where the hunter-gatherer instincts of some of us result in an extravagant basketful of crayfish and scallops for all.

It's before eight o'clock in the morning and the phone rings:

"Good morning! Are your tanks filled?" comes the all-too-breezy voice from the coast (we're not always the best early-risers).

But we're half expecting the call, the sun is shining and the day is calm.   "We're all ready, and the dive kit is in the car" we lie, as we leap into action, and, as ever, wish we'd written ourselves a checklist that would make putting all the essentials together at breakneck speed so much easier.

"So where are we diving today?" I ask.

"The usual spot!" comes the evasive reply.

The phone may be tapped, the crayfish may be gone before we get there unless we take extreme precautions. We lug the kit into the boot of the car, the dogs running around us with a mixture of excitement mixed with bitter disappointment as they cotton on to the realisation that this is a trip on which they will not be invited. Bob always seems to know, but for the other two, the truth always dawns too late. So the day starts early, and somewhat tide dependent. The boat will be launched, and all those who are keen to do some diving will be whisked out into the bay at high speed. The location is a poorly guarded secret, there are too many people living here for any hidden natural larders, but everyone pretends that they know of one last place where nobody else goes, where the crayfish are still abundant, but we still hear the oft-repeated phrase:

"I could tell you where I found them, but then I'd have to kill you."

After a couple of dives for crayfish and scallops, and with the onshore breeze starting to blow, we zoom homewards, bouncing over the chop, exhausted and exhilarated. The spoils are assessed, and the phone calls will go out depending on the quantity of the catch. Most will arrive by car, but occasionally a tiny distant speck, glimmering out in the bay, will reveal itself as a small boat and a family will arrive in a more romantic transportation, before pondering on the more practical issues such as when will the tide come in enough to leave again? They may even have to punish themselves with an enforced overnight stay. These feasts are legendary in their own small way, and as long as we all muck in with the delicate process of preparing the delicious and messy sea creatures, and as long as there's plenty of wine to keep us going, the afternoon will glide into the evening. The fire will be lit, the candles will glow and the darkness will find us replete and smug. The conversation expands to fill the available space, encompassing the blinking lights of Russell, the last glow of the distant clouds in the east. Eventually the dazzling stars appear as the Milky Way unfolds above us. And we'll wonder, collectively, how much our lives have been changed by this discovery for us of a place that is at once both familiar and exotic, mapped and yet rare, and too far away from the great herds of population to have become a distant memory of what it used to be.

Once, long ago, much of the north Mediterranean

coastline would have felt like this, warm, secure, and untroubled. And no doubt, one distant day, this place will be as chewed up and spat out as the rest of the world, but for now, and who knows for how long, peace still reverberates silently around this coast, lulling us to contentment in its gentle warmth.

Rugby

There used to be a time in New Zealand's not too distant past, that part of history that they describe here as "back in the day", when rugby was the national religion. Whilst there is still an intense enthusiasm for the sport, it's no longer heresy to admit that you might have missed the All Blacks match last night. Having said that, participation in the game at any level is still taken very seriously, and every match, from the smallest club match to the international test matches will draw some sort of crowd. The village in which we are fortunate enough to live has an excellent pitch, well looked after, and floodlit for those late winter fixtures. We were surprised to discover that the local team is very highly regarded, having supplied New Zealand, over the years, with several All Blacks. I say surprised with some justification, the village is only seven hundred people strong. The enthusiasm for the game is reflected in the spectators, so we went along to a local match to cheer on our newly adopted favourite team. It was superb!

About a third of the village was gathered on the sidelines. The field is wide enough that everyone can park their cars facing the pitch, and the smaller people could look over the heads of the taller by sitting on the roof of the car. There was a great feeling of camaraderie amongst the supporters, and everyone was very welcoming, especially as we were so new to the village. Whether or not our team won (I really don't recall) the atmosphere was one of great enjoyment.

That I can't remember who won may be a cause for concern;. I have met many sports fans who seem to be able to carry around in their memory vast databases of statistical information about their chosen subject. I regret to say that I'm not a true fan in that way, but I really love the atmosphere of the live game.

Later that month, the All Blacks were playing against the Wallabies, the Australian national team, at Eden Park in Auckland, so we had to go and watch that! Five of us drove down to Auckland and piled into a small, comfortable apartment near the top of Queen's Street. The weather gradually got worse and wetter as evening approached, and by the time we were heading off to Britomart and the train to Eden Park, the rain was torrential, and the sky had gone all black. We bought some huge black dustbin liners, put holes in them for the head, and wore them as team-coloured wet weather gear. Despite the downpour, the stadium was packed, and the atmosphere fizzing.

Appetising, but surprisingly unpleasant hot dogs and coldish beer were the refreshments for the match, so my memory of the game was tempered with a chronic wish for some antacid relief but, despite the indigestion and the water running down my glasses, the match was excellent. We weren't close to the pitch, so much of the detail was easier seen on the big TV screen over the far goalposts, and I'm sure that we'd have had a much better view of the match at home on TV, but that's not the point; being at the stadium gives so much more feeling. I do remember that the All Blacks won this time, but I also remember the bizarre shouts of some of the crowd around us just as well,

"Play it towards the cheap seats!" and "kill him!" seemed to ring out at regular intervals, as if a parrot had learnt a new phrase.

The crowd around us were definitely there for the fun of the event at least as much as for watching the match, and frequent good-natured insults flew back and forth. I don't think I've ever stood outside in such heavy rain in my life, and truthfully, I think the black bin bags were probably as wet on the inside from condensation, but gradually that rain stopped, and after the match we all admitted that there is a quality of memory that comes with an event like this that is irreplaceable. The chaos after the match as everyone left the ground was extraordinary. I have no idea how we managed to catch a bus, never mind stay on our feet, the crowd was so dense, but we seemed to swiftly be transported into town, all together and still high from the shared experience. I think we might have inadvertently been pushed to the front of a queue, but nobody seemed to notice or care, and everyone was in high spirits except the grumpy bus drivers. They would probably have preferred to be spectators, too.

Oddly, bearing in mind that about twenty thousand people were descending on Auckland on a Saturday at about half past ten at night, there were very few places left open for food and drink in the centre. In that way, the city definitely has a little of the provincial town feel about it, despite appearances. We did eventually find somewhere that had remained open but they seemed a little bemused that we might want to eat at such a late hour.

With all that in mind, I was really intrigued to see how New Zealand would prepare itself for the Rugby World Cup in 2011. Would the most enthusiastic rugby nation in the world do itself justice off the field? Following the damp squib that was Auckland after the international we saw, I didn't have high hopes, and when the government of the day decided that the major stadium in Auckland, at Eden Park, just needed new seating (for a few million dollars!) rather than an entirely new venue on the waterfront (for a few million more) I really felt that the chances of the country throwing a world famous rugby party were slim. I was delighted to be proved wrong. Northland hosted three of the international teams, Canada, Japan and Tonga. All three have red and white flags and, for a month before the tournament started, much of Northland had become emblazoned in pennants of red and white.

The hospitality was amazing. A chance encounter on a domestic flight between the Canadian coach and a local farmer led to a huge and impromptu party for many locals and the Canadian squad. Many schools hosted the teams and became dual-nationality supporters, and generally an enormous generosity of spirit allowed all the foreign teams to feel part of something quite special. It really did seem that the hype the politicians had promoted, that of a "stadium of four million supporters" was not far from the truth.

New buildings started to spring up on Auckland's waterfront, and a whole new area, peppered with bars, restaurants and big screens, became a magnet for the influx of visitors both foreign and local. Promotion of New Zealand's culture, both western and Maori, became a matter of pride and endless punditry and by the time of the opening ceremony, not just Auckland, but the whole country was agog.

In fact, so agog were we, that the organisers of the event completely underestimated the crowds. A wharf that had been designated "Party Central" by the people who designate these things, was full in about ten minutes. The overflow areas overflowed. Public transport choked and stood still. The council anticipated about twenty thousand revellers, but over one hundred thousand people turned up to revel. Some of them had to go home, and some of them never got to the match, but the overwhelming consensus was that it had been a massive success. The council rushed to ensure that the transport and accommodation of the opening night were not a problem at the following nights, and pretty much got it right thereafter. And for the weeks of the actual matches, despite a sense of over-saturation that comes with monomania, New Zealand showed the world that it was capable of putting on a huge party. It had none of the glamour of the Beijing Olympics, and cost a relatively small amount, but for those people who were touched by it in any way, it was seen as a delightful triumph, friendly, welcoming and upbeat. Not unlike the persona of the host nation.

That the All Blacks won the final didn't hurt too much. The funny thing was, nobody seems to know how they'd feel if they had lost. It was so unthinkable that nobody had considered it.

Swimming with Dolphins

One of the aspects of the Bay of Islands that I really love is the abundance of wildlife, and the pristine nature of the area. I know that those whose families have lived here for generations will tell me that a generation ago there were many more fish, birds, trees and beaches, and that everything is spoiled, but I can only report what I see, and it is this. On any European coast with the same climate, this bay would, during the last hundreds of years, have become heavily populated, built up and over-fished. Whilst it might have retained its geographical charms, it would have lost its fauna and flora to the advancing tide of humans.

I think that the Bay is a jewel of a place, still teeming with fish, seabirds, and a whole ecosystem that supports itself. This is what environmentalists call 'the sliding baseline', by which they mean that the definition of normal will depend upon our own experience. On a boat trip in the bay you will often encounter a pod of dolphins, keeping their distance, but never running too far away. Occasionally, we might even see an orca or two, although rarely. Commercial companies take tourists on dolphin-watching trips and even promise that they will see these fleet cetaceans or be given a refund.

One beautiful day on a September weekend, it was a bit early in the spring for much swimming but it happened to be Wayne's's birthday, so with several friends, we took a trip in his boat out to Deepwater Cove, which used to be one of our favourite spots for catching crayfish (it's now a marine reserve). The diving was reasonable, I only caught one crayfish of edible size and another friend, Ralph, who doesn't like diving but loves fishing, caught a snapper. Wayne, as usual when he dives, caught enough for everyone else, so we were pretty happy about that, and looking forward to the excellent seafood that we've become so accustomed to.

I'd only just hauled myself onto the boat and Laura was still in the water when Guy called out:

"You've just missed a pod of dolphins swimming around the boat!". What a disappointment not to have seen them, but we were sure they'd be back another day. Suddenly, we were startled to see a gleaming fin break the surface only a few metres away, then another. Laura stayed in the water with snorkel and mask, as did Guy. Wayne's eldest daughter simply leapt off the boat, with lifejacket and jeans still on in her teenage enthusiasm for a chance to swim with them!

There were about fifteen dolphins, all really content to make some sort of contact, and a couple of young ones amongst them. They came very close to the swimmers, well within reach but playfully darting away, only to return seconds later. I grabbed the camera and tried endless permutations of second guessing the movements of these lovely animals, but managed nothing more than hundreds of pictures of sparkling water, occasionally punctured by a fin or a snorkel. Even from the boat, I could hear the whistles and clicks of the dolphins as they chatted to each other, and it couldn't have been warning sounds, they seemed to want to be there as much as we did. I kept thinking I'd jump in too, the opportunity seemed too good to miss but, at the same time, I really wanted to get a photograph of this amazing event, and I felt certain that, any minute now, the dolphins would swim away, leaving me wondering why I bothered.

In the end, the dolphins stayed near the boat and the swimmers for about ninety minutes, making warning gestures by slapping the water with their tail flukes when the young ones became isolated, and then playful ones when they were all together again. It's impossible to know what they were getting out of this brief communication, but probably much the same as we were. The chance to interact in play with another species is rare and precious and the moment was just pure serendipity.

Laura's Trousers

When it rains here, it rains a deluge. Not for nothing are the paddocks as green as they are, all year round. The rainwater for most rural households is collected in tanks for drinking and all the other things for which water is generally needed. This means that the roofs have to be sound, the guttering (spouting as it is called here) free from leaves and birds nests, and designed so that the abundant rain doesn't go to waste.

We hadn't been here long when we encountered the first big downpour. At this point our roof was an entirely unknown quantity, and not even something we'd thought much about. That's the thing with roofs, you take them for granted until it pours with rain. Well, it wasn't entirely watertight, and by the time the rain had fallen for a day, there was a line of pans and bowls across a corner of the kitchen, with the rhythmic and soothing harmony of plops and tings as they slowly filled. The next day the rain was showing no intention of abating, and I went off to work. As a result, I had no idea of the mini-drama unfolding back home. What I did know was that the rain had been pounding in town all day, and the daylight had been little better than twilight.

I arrived home expecting the usual array of drop-catching receptacles in the kitchen, but I didn't expect to see my lovely wife's bottom in the kitchen window. Earlier that afternoon, and with a suddenness and ferocity that startled her (actually, that tells you little, Laura is rather easier to startle than an agoraphobic doe) water started pouring down the outside of the kitchen window by the bucketful. Swift intervention was required. The window frame was not in the best of shape and water could soon start pouring into the kitchen units, so Laura grabbed a stepladder, threw on a waterproof coat and went out to investigate. Somehow the downpipe had become blocked and the water had rapidly backed up along the gutter until it could only overflow and escape down the wall and window. Precariously perched on the top step, Laura reckoned she could temporarily rig a small piece of corrugated iron over the gutter so that it would divert the water away from the side of the house, at least until the rain had subsided enough that we could clean out the gutter and pipes and fix the problem. It was a balancing act. Iron sheet in one hand, step of the ladder in the other, rain blasting down and no spare hand for...trousers. So, of course, soaked by the deluge, they responded to the demands of gravity and that's when I arrived home, just in time for Laura to discover that, by grasping the top of the downpipe for support, the blockage in the gutter miraculously drained away and cleared. And just in time for me to see my wife's near naked bum at the kitchen window on the wettest day we'd had since we arrived. Just another unforgettable memory of something that would never have happened to us in our urban past.

Pig's Head Road

The Northland deluge of March 2007 left many roads devastated and impassable due to landslides. They said it was a 'one in 150-year storm'. But what do they know? Three months later there was another one of similar ferocity. The speed at which the repairs to the roads were completed is an achievement borne of necessity, but near miraculous, nevertheless. Within a month all the roads that we were in the habit of using were back to normal and, whilst there were still large scars of red-ochre clay on steeply sided hills, the roads had all been fixed, or so we thought.

On a fine crisp day in May we decided to take the dogs for a scenic drive across to Russell by the old road. This is a long drive involving, as it does, a drive south for nearly an hour before turning eastward towards the coast. We had barely hit the dirt road when we encountered signs that the Russell old road was still closed, over two months after the floods. There was, however, a detour, down a little-used route called Pig's Head Road. So we took it, and what a delight it was. It plunged us almost straight away into a narrow, steeply sloping valley, the hilltops heavily wooded, the lower lying areas occupied by mature and well managed farmland and the road lined with enormous and majestic macrocarpas. And beyond, in the far distance, sudden glimpses of the turquoise sea, often at unexpected angles as if it were sloping, by some suspension of the usual rules of gravity.

As an aside, I have to say something about Macrocarpas here. In Northland, fast growing, dense and hardy, they have been used as a windbreak tree. Planted in a close row they do form a very dense shelter-belt, it's true, but plant one of these trees in splendid isolation and the Monterey Cypress (Cupressus Macrocarpa), as the tree is otherwise known, shows its full glory. They grow tall, perhaps forty metres in a good specimen, often with multiple trunks, and a most majestic profile. They are, without doubt, one of the most beautiful of all the softwood trees, and it is almost an insult to them to use as a hedge!

But now, back to the tale. Farmhouses scattered at intervals along the road all had similar characteristics; they were old, villa style buildings, well used and well cared-for, and the valley had a really magical feel. A tractor hove into sight ahead of us, and we slowed to its pace as there was no room to pass. As the farmer pulled off to the verge and waved us past, we noticed with delight that not only was the tractor painted a shocking pink, but the elderly driver was dressed in pink dungarees and shirt. This is obviously a valley that cares well for its eccentrics. He waved and smiled, we waved back. This brief and cheery encounter served to put a grin on our faces for the rest of the day. The road wound its way towards the coast becoming more of a switchback, with ever more frequent views of the sea and then, suddenly, there we were, on the coast at the beautiful, completely deserted (it was way out of season) Teal Bay. A small settlement of holiday baches crowded the waterfront, all closed up and sleeping and a dairy, positioned perfectly for passing trade as well as local needs, was thankfully open. The drive had taken longer than expected, and the obligatory New Zealand pie was definitely going to be lunch. Mmm, steak and cheese!

Bob and Brodie too were delighted (this was in the days before Talulah had joined us). They could hear the breaking surf through the closed window of the Jeep from about five hundred metres away, and the proximity of the beach was too much for their patience to bear. So, pie in hand (and face and lap and footwell) we drove to the water for vigorous stick-throwing activities.

Once the boys were thoroughly tired out, it was time to press on northwards. There are some lovely, tiny secluded beaches in this bit of coast, just around the southern tip of Cape Brett and, had time been a willing accomplice, we would have stopped at them all. But Russell, by this route, was still a long way off, so we drove on. There was a great feeling of comfort to be had in the knowledge that these pretty bays were not going anywhere, and we could return to do more exploring whenever the mood took us. So we didn't feel any sense of loss when driving past so many picture-perfect little inlets, making a mental note of their location, and promising ourselves a return visit before too long. (Months later, we did, indeed take the road out this way once more. And thanks to attempting to depend entirely on memory for navigation, we became hopelessly lost, turned around, lost, found and lost again).

In time, we rejoined the tarmac road, and drew near to Russell. Suddenly, what had seemed like a magical adventure all day became a little mundane. A brief glance at each other:

"Have we had enough of the exploring yet?"

We answered each other

"No!"

So we drove past Russell and on to Rawhiti. Rawhiti is the last stop on the road that follows the southern coastline of the Bay of Islands. It's a very pretty settlement in a typically attractive bay, sparsely populated, beautiful, perfect, and, on that day hot (for May) and sunny. There was just time for the dogs to have another quick dip, capture them on film (of course we'll keep saying "film" for a few years yet!) and then head back the rutted road to Russell for a quick stop and a spot of liquid refreshment, a brief drive to the ferry across to Opua and a then, before the sleepy dogs started to wonder where their next meal was coming from, short drive home. And oddly, thanks to the friendly wave from the pink-clad farmer of Pig's Head Road, the day was a highlight, and an unexpected detour became a most memorable adventure on the back-roads.

The Local

You're in a small town in a rural area. You're new to the area. There's a local pub, or hotel as they're called here. It looks quite old fashioned and as well worn as the rest of the village. The cars parked outside and the music drifting towards you tell you that you're not going to be the only customers there tonight. In fact, it looks quite popular. You and your friends walk in to the bar, and what happens? Of course, the hubbub of conversation stops, the locals swivel in your direction, and someone accidentally drops a very noisy pin. At least it sounds noisy. You pause, wonder if you should have just gone to the off-licence and then, back-footed, brave the scowling barman who reminds you, as if you needed it, that you are not a local.

This is exactly what didn't happen to us when we first visited the local hotel. Back in Scotland, and perhaps unusually, we were not big fans of pubs and bars. We were more likely to visit them as a local place to eat rather than for a drinking session, so we felt it unlikely that we'd miss the traditional rural pub coming to New Zealand, even though there are some as it turns out. But we still wanted to visit our local hotel. We'd driven past it many times when we first arrived, and seen it boarded up with red and white emergency services tape across the doors and "unsafe-keep out!" signs about the place. A disgruntled tenant had damaged the place in a fit of arson apparently, and a bit of a rebuild was needed. Not many months later it was back open with a shiny new lick of paint, of a hue so intense, that it can now be seen from outer space (but now, thanks to Google Earth, so can everything else). We walked in, hoping to remain reasonably discreet, knowing few neighbours at this point, and were rewarded with several very cheery "hellos!" and offers of drinks. We could not have been made more welcome, and I'm sure that this was nothing to do with us being new residents to the area. Few people there knew we were living locally. It's just plain friendly here! Within minutes we were embroiled in a game of pool with two extremely large Maori guys who were very well travelled, wanted to know where we had come from, where we were going to, and (for a change) what we thought of New Zealand.

It was so easy to feel a sense of belonging, and I'm sure our sense of euphoria at such an effortless adoption was not just down to the beer. There must be something they put in the water. The bar itself was a combination of very old fashioned woodwork, etched glass and mirrors, very modern, the electronic squeals and chirps of the pokies (fruit machines) which are a standard feature of the hotels throughout the country) and the furniture from all eras and styles. It wasn't and still isn't a pretty place, but it is functional, cheerful and popular. So why change it? The village is so small that the hotel is the centre of activities by default, and functions as a meeting place and village hall as much as a watering hole.

Run, Rabbit.

The summer of the drought wore on. There were many benefits that flowed from the dependable sunshine, not least the predictable barbecue, and the certainty of boating at the weekend. But the rabbit population flourished and the hedonistic bunnies managed to squeeze an additional breeding season into their routine. So now we had a plague of them. Not on the level that you might see on historic films of the Australian outback, but certainly a noticeable increase. Tree roots were dug up, holes appeared around fence posts, and the cats had scratched little rabbit icons on the doorframe near the catflap in the style of WWII dogfight aces.

I decided I should learn how to control these pests by shooting them. I mean, you can't live in the countryside, pretend to be a gentleman farmer, and not own a gun. The first part of the process was to apply for a firearms licence. This involved some minor paperwork, an interview with a police officer, references from those that know me best (so lovely wife and misguided friend), and an exam to pass, based on common sense. Which, when it comes to firearms, still exists! A cheque to the relevant department, and the credit-card sized piece of plastic is mine. (I wonder who decided on the size of the credit card, and thank heavens they had common sense. If a bureaucrat had made that decision, we might have ended up with A4 wallets).

A gun safe is mandatory, a suitable locked box in which the rifle must be kept, so we asked our joiner friend to build something. The police inspector was impressed. So now I was all ready. However, I didn't go out and buy a gun. The temptation was there, and the allure of the hunting shop with its technical discussion and research, muzzle velocities, choice of round, barrel finish, telescopic sights, and so much more to think about was beckoning. For many men, this kind of decision making is a delight in itself. And any women who love a fine shoe shop would understand immediately. And, no doubt, vice-versa too.

I would have really liked to go and buy that gun. I'm a reasonable shot, with a steady hand, and an ability to focus on the task in hand, but they're not a cheap item, and I didn't want the rifle to be sitting in the gun safe, and never be used. So I borrowed a good airgun from a friend, not as powerful as the rimfire rifle I had in mind, but certainly enough to kill a bunny cleanly. The gun then went in the safe. Any opportunity I had for a wander round the paddocks with the gun, I would take, and see if I could get close enough to a rabbit.

After about four months, I had one rabbit in the freezer. Not exactly a cull. So what am I doing wrong? I chatted to friends, I looked online and I realised that wandering around the paddocks with a gun was not going to encourage the bunnies within range. What I really needed to be doing was hiding myself in amongst the favourite playgrounds for the rabbits. And wait. And then wait a little more. And probably wait a bit longer, too. A high-intensity light would also help, as the rabbits tend to do a lot of their overground foraging when the light is dim. I decided that once spring was in the air, I would take to the shelter belt with all the supplies I needed for an evening's entertainment: gun, stool, torch, flask (and fly repellent – those sandflies always start to celebrate the return of spring).

Waimate North Show

In 1842, when the treaty of Waitangi was only two years old, and the Pakeha settlers from Europe were only staring to come to terms with the responsibilities they had taken on, an agricultural demonstration was held on some farmland at Te Waimate, one of the oldest colonial settlements in New Zealand. The purpose of the demonstration was to help some of the new arrivals to the colonies to familiarise themselves with the counter-intuitive march of the seasons, the unexpected warmth and humidity of the North, and the suitability of crops and animals for farming here.

Every year since then, there has been an agricultural show at Waimate North, and the event has blossomed into a huge country fair, with livestock demonstrations, baking, produce and art competitions and, more recently, a whole section devoted to the wine and food of Northland. There are wood chopping competitions, craft stalls, bars, and children's entertainments. There are agricultural equipment stands, and even car and boat sales. Hundreds of people are drawn to the showgrounds, and the atmosphere in such a beautiful pastoral setting, is a delight.

We've established, in the comparatively short time

we've been here, a tradition all of our own that accompanies the show. We arrive at breakfast time at the house of some friends that overlooks the showgrounds and, along with about twenty others, we feast on breakfast pastries, bacon and pies, all washed down with sparkling wine and fresh juice. Then, slightly tipsy, we roll down the hill to the show and wander around, taking in the amazing display of livestock, the brilliant little stand with the small animals for sale (this is Laura's favourite) where we can see ducklings, chicks, lambs and kids, and plan our next venture into animal obsession! The craft stands are packed and fantastic, the woodchopping breathtaking (and slightly terrifying - I have no idea how anyone can attack a chunk of wood with an axe at that speed and not accidentally hack themselves into small pieces as well), and the equipment stands are like a modern museum of shiny farming gear. Never again will that tractor look as new!

When we're full of the looking, and the sun is taking its toll (it always seems to be sunny on the second Saturday in November), the tent with the best of the produce from Northland beckons. Wine tasting (with show-only bargains!) and savoury treats herald lunchtime, and the hardest part is to decide what to eat and when to stop drinking. It's impossible to move more than ten metres without bumping into friends, and an impromptu picnic always ensues. By now the combination of sun, food and

Bacchus has insisted that we sit down somewhere and it's bound to be within range of the big truck that is the stage for the singing competition. The standard of entry, mainly children, is amazingly high, and this has become a very popular event. The performances can elicit rapturous applause.

By now it might be time to visit the old show hall. The hall was built in 1891, and hasn't been altered since then, so it's very old by New Zealand standards. Inside, it feels as if it might have been like this at every show for over 100 years; the cakes and preserves beautifully displayed, the fine specimens of home-grown veggies in museum-like perfection, and an abundance of local arts and crafts from local people of all ages adorn the slightly dusty, musty hall. We wander around, and promise ourselves that next year, we'll enter some of the categories, whilst at the same time wondering if our produce, our preserving, and our artiness are up to the high standard that is clearly evident here.

Blinking, we return to the bright outdoors, and make a final run around the stalls, catching up on acquaintances and friends in the process, before bidding the show a final farewell until next year, and retreating home before the traffic rush begins. For the rest of the evening, the road outside our house hums to the sound of departing crowds and traffic, and the show has laid down another year of tradition and patina.

Shabby Chic

Laura and Millie have much in common. They are dynamic, persuasive and lovely. They also have extremely similar taste in design and living environments and, if things are not as they'd like, then just give them five minutes, because that's how long it takes for a complete refurbishment, whether it's the re-covering of an old couch, or (even as I write this) the redecoration of a room. When they both realised that their tastes coincided to such a degree, it didn't take them long to decide it was imperative that they should open a shop as an outlet for these skills. And suddenly, 'Shabby Chic' was born. I think that took about five minutes, too.

Phase one was to visit as many car-boot and garage sales as possible to locate the raw materials for the stock. This was no hardship, I think that they'd do this by preference at the drop of a hat. Similarly, trademe.co.nz was ruthlessly plundered for items that were in need of their special attention. Within a month, with frantic painting, sanding, gluing and covering, an extraordinary range of items had been resurrected from tired retirement to country cottage glory.

Then came phase two. The local landlord of a bar and restaurant in the best location in Kerikeri had a blacksmith's shed that could be converted into a shop; a promotional stall just for one day at the Waimate North show would set the ball rolling. The show day arrived, and with a trailer and several cars laden with the fruits of the months of labour aboard, we set up stall at some unearthly hour. Only the bacon sandwich stall was open for business (actually, that's all we needed). Our stall looked superb, like a feature in a magazine devoted to country living, even the bunting was hand-made. The show opened at nine o'clock. By half past ten everything (that's absolutely everything) had sold. The stall was a roaring success, but it highlighted one serious flaw in the business model. It took a lot of work to make a day's worth of stock.

It took a few more days for the shop to open. More furniture had been located, decorated and distressed. The smithy had been cleaned and painted. The day was sunny and the flyers had been distributed, and a sense of deja-vu had been delivered. Within the first hour or so of opening, almost everything had been sold, much of it to the same person. As a model of successful marketing, turnover and cashflow, the shop was an instant hit. As a business, not so much. Both Laura and Millie were hoping that this would be a gentle, and fairly casual way of indulging in their passion and skill for resurrecting the ordinary to the level of sublime, but instead, its own success made it a millstone. Neither of them wanted to find themselves in constant demand in the shop, and their vision of maybe selling the occasional piece to keep the shop ticking over became replaced by the memory of a queue of ardent customers requesting one-off bespoke pieces to fit their homes.

And so, despite phone calls from prospective customers asking when the little shop would be open next, their love of the restoration of items of beauty returned to the domestic level, and the shop was no more.

Now Then

Several years have passed since I started writing this account of our move to New Zealand. It's not healthy or kind to ask friends and family whether we have changed much since we moved but, strictly in the spirit of research and with no regard for a potentially inflamed ego, the question has to be asked. So, has our move changed us? Of course the answer is yes and no. We are still the same people (albeit not one red blood corpuscle is older than one hundred and twenty days, so exceptions must be made) and any changes to us are subtle. We're more open to new experiences and ideas since arriving here, This is an essential ingredient of migration, in my view, and is the lubricant that greases the easing into a new way of life (oh, the metaphor!).

We are distinctly calmer. Others have observed this about us, it's not a subjective assessment. We must have been as tense as a Soviet-era weightlifter at a drug test when we were here for our initial look-around, because it was the defining quality that our friends noticed disappearing in us over the months. It's funny, we knew we were under stress then, but we didn't feel uncomfortably anxious, just keen to start our new plans. We were out today having a coffee and, at a nearby table, sat a couple who were on and off their mobile phones on a regular basis. Their faces were pale and lined and the telephone conversations were tense and heated. Laura said:

"That was what we looked like a few years ago."

Now we are deeply tanned, muscular and carefree, with long flowing locks, a surfboard under one arm, and a fishing rod under the other. Which makes for awkward handshakes. We are certainly more content, and this is most gratifying. If there is one criterion that would define the move here a success, it would be a sense of contentment, a decrease in the notion of life being just an endless sequence of wants, either met and forgotten or unrequited and worrying away just under the surface.

One thing that has changed, and probably the one that I was hoping for the most, is the opportunity for the long lunch. In my dreams, this was at a long narrow table, where the food, drink and atmosphere are courtesy of the Mediterranean cliché. This requires a warm, preferably sunny day, much homegrown produce and several bottles of wine. It requires the presence of friends in expansive mood, and preferably representing at least three generations. Well, these have become a major feature of our weekend life. The venue and the time of day may vary, but the atmosphere of conviviality, epicurean delight and that unhurried pace of relaxation is always there. I don't care that we look like some set for an olive oil advert, it's our life and it's what we love!

One of Laura's main concerns about living so far from Scotland was suddenly being so far from her small but close family. I have lived away from the rest of my family for years, but Laura was used to seeing her brother frequently, and her mum and dad were always in touch if not closer. In this regard, technology is a really wonderful thing. The Apple Mac is a friendly computer and the webcam that accompanies it is nothing short of brilliant. With a little bit of planning by email, and a small amount of crossing of fingers, (because we live in the present, not in the distant future where everything technological is always reliable) Laura's parents are virtually in the kitchen, chatting away, sharing jokes. Even the comfortable silences that are such a feature of family conversations are reproduced across the thousands of kilometres. With the webcam on the laptop, we can even walk around the garden, inspect the produce, and greet the dogs! Because the connection is broadband and inexpensive, there's no time constraint, and none of the tricky "this must be costing you a fortune" comments that can so often be a hindrance to a good chat. I never thought that the internet would be as practical and functional as this.

Cricket by Candlelight

We've come a long way from the fast car on the winding road from Glasgow. The couple you can see looking tanned (or is it just weather-beaten?) and relaxed, sitting on their deck surrounded by the soft Northland countryside are barely recognisable as the pasty and taut-faced urbanites of a few years ago. If someone had told us that we'd sell everything, move across the world, set up a new life and be happier than we could imagine, we might possibly have believed them, but the sheer weight of inertia we were carrying would have made the idea of the move seem impossible, or at the least, very unlikely.

It really wasn't until we reached a crisis point, before motivation started to kick in and the future began to drag us towards it. And it really did feel like that. With only the smallest amount of hindsight, it was as if we were already here, living this life, and all our stressed-out city-dwelling selves needed to do was to wander into the future, pour themselves a long drink, and join us on the deck. If our lives hadn't been in such a stressful state in the UK, we might never had made the journey.

One lovely still day, we had just returned from a brief visit to the UK for Laura's brother's wedding and were feeling happy to be back. We'd missed our friends, so we invited them to join us for a long, relaxed evening. As is traditional here when a group of us gather to eat, everyone brought a plate of food, and an instant feast was in the offing. However the children (our friends' kids) were hoping for something more energetic. So whilst we ate and drank, chatted and laughed, the kids set up a very informal game of cricket on the lawn under the great old oak tree. Time rolled by and the wine flowed, darkness slowly fell, and the children, rather than having to stop the game, collected candles in jam-jars and set them out on the grass so that the game could continue in the half-light, looking for all the world like an entirely contrived but beautifully illuminated scene from a Peter Greenaway film.

We paused in our light-hearted chatter and looked towards the old oak tree, the children and the candlelight. The night air was warm and still, and perhaps we had drunk a little too much wine.

"That might be the most wonderful thing I've ever seen." I mused, possibly aloud.

But we were all captivated by the sight, a modern rendering of an old-master painting, the flickering light, the animated and chaotic game, and the feeling that a perfect moment had been unveiled before our eyes. And sure, it may have looked like the most clichéd expression of colonialism, and I wouldn't have put it together that way on purpose, but that night, with its good company, hilarious conversation (unrepeatable before the watershed), lovely food, still spring air and the distant laughter and enthusiastic shouting of children, was uniquely ours, and uniquely home.

The end.

For photographs, more information, and a link to Laura's blog, please visit: lloydjerome.com

www.ingramcontent.com/pod-product-compliance
Ingram Content Group UK Ltd.
Pitfield, Milton Keynes, MK11 3LW, UK
UKHW041431210726
13854UKWH00010B/1850